I Remember Like Now: The Odyssey of a Polish Jew

I Remember Like Now:

The Odyssey of a Polish Jew

by Chaim Goldberg

as told to Jo Atkinson

Edited by Jo Atkinson and Colin Atkinson

BMP

Black Moss Press

Published by:

(BMP) Black Moss Press
2450 Byng Rd., Windsor, Ont. N8W 3E8.

Black Moss Press books are published with the assistance of the Canada Council, the Ontario Arts Council and the Department of Communications (Heritage Canada).

Distribution for Black Moss in Canada and the U.S. is handled by:
Firefly Books, 250 Sparks St., Willowdale, Ont. M2H 2S4.
All orders should be directed there.

Book design by Benchmark Publishing & Design, Windsor, Ont.

Canadian Cataloguing in Publication Data

Goldberg, Chaim, 1920-

I remember like now: the odyssey of a Polish Jew

ISBN 0-88753-239-X

1. Goldberg, Chaim, 1920- . 2. Jews. Polish–Biography. 3. World War, 1939-1945–Personal narratives, Polish. 4. World War, 1939-1945–Personal narratives, Jewish. 5. World War, 1939-1945–Biography. I. Atkinson, Jo II. Title.

D811.G63 1994 940.54'81438 C94-900389-1

This book is dedicated to the Goldberg
family, only a few of whom survived.

– C.G.

And to the memory of my father.

– J.A.

Table of Contents

Introduction

Early in the morning of September 1, 1939, without warning, Hitler invaded Poland. On September 6th, Chaim Goldberg, a nineteen-year-old fur worker, left Warsaw on foot and slowly made his way to Vilna, while the Germans bombed indiscriminately and the Red Army marched in from the east. *I Remember Like Now* is the adventures of a Polish Jew whose unique voice recreates the thoughts and feelings of an unselfconscious, resourceful young workingman in a time of confusion and horror. Chaim Goldberg was neither victim nor hero, but an ordinary person coping with extraordinary events.

His style captures the humorous ironies of Yiddish, and the book is the record of a spoken narrative. I made the editorial decision to try to capture the experience of listening to him tell his story in his own voice. Therefore I retained his idioms, such as "mine captain" and "keeped," which derive from his first language, Yiddish. To rework his narrative in standard English would destroy the immediacy of his voice and lose the force of his personality. He is uncomplaining and matter-of-fact: he always thought he'd return to Warsaw "but it never happened"; he figured "the German Army would come in and *behave like an army*." Living in Vilna on forged documents, fearful of being drafted into Stalin's army, he applied to the NKVD–"the worst ones, the only time when they worked was twelve o'clock at night"–for permission to cross the Soviet Union to Japan, as he made his way toward his overwhelming dream of seeing the Germans defeated.

After the war, he moved far from Poland where all his family had perished and returned to an ordinary life, in Canada. He married, and opened Hy's Fish Shop in Windsor, Ontario–"If it swims, it's at Hy's." For years I had bought my fish there, but had never thought of him as having been an adventurous, even daring, young man. After learning his story, I wondered: "How would I have acted, given the extraordinary circumstances he had lived through?" As a hard-working man, father of three educated and successful sons, with eleven grandchildren, even he now finds his earlier life, which he remembers "like now," hard to believe.

Jo Atkinson

Acknowledgments

I certainly could not have done this book without the help of those in the Inter-Library Loan Office and the Reference Department of the Leddy Library at the University of Windsor: I thank Janice Bell and Maureen Souchuk of Inter-Library Loan; and Bob Elliott, Lou-Anne Greenham, Bill Jackson, Graham Staffen, and Ana-Maria Sydor of Reference. I also thank Kai Hildebrandt and Susan Wendt-Hildebrandt for their help with the German phrases; John Barker for help with military ranks and terms; and Ron Welch and Chandran Fernando for help with maps.

Historical Background

The Poles are a Slavic people whose homeland has its origins some time before the tenth century, when the Poles became Christians. The boundaries expanded and contracted throughout the Middle Ages as the Poles battled various neighbours to gain or regain land. After uniting with Lithuania in 1569, Poland became the largest state in eastern Europe, eventually becoming the most multi-cultural country in all Europe.

Feudalism was never instituted in Poland, that is, the gentry *(schlachta)* did not hold their land from the monarch. In the sixteenth century, the schlachta forced an elective monarchy on the country, and during succeeding years they grew in power at the expense of a centralized monarchy. In part because of the *liberum veto* (the rule that no law could be passed without unanimity among members of the Seym *[Parliament]*), by the eighteenth century, Poland had become weak, vulnerable, and virtually ungovernable. The monarchs of Prussia, Austria, and Russia took advantage of this weakness, and took chunks of the country in 1772 and 1793, and in 1795 they made a final partition, completely eliminating the country.

Napoleon set up the Grand Duchy of Warsaw in 1807 on areas taken from Prussian and Austrian Poland. Polish hopes of independence were revived. Napoleon marched on Moscow with 85,000 Polish volunteer soldiers in his army. After he was defeated, Poland was again partitioned at the Congress of Vienna in 1815, the Tsar adding all of the Duchy to his Polish holdings. Once more the country disappeared, but the Poles never gave in, and revolted valiantly though unsuccessfully, especially in 1831, 1848, and 1861, the last rebellion taking three years to crush.

At the end of World War I, in the chaos and civil war which followed the collapse of the Austrian, Prussian, and Russian empires and the Russian Revolution, Poles once more fought for nationhood. Under the brilliant General Joseph Pilsudski, the Polish Legions defeated the new Red Army. After the war, Poland was reconstituted but was half the size it had been before the Partitions. Polish leaders had no illusion that the independence of their new state was secure. German leaders in the 1920s and Soviet leaders in the 1930s were hostile, echoing German General von Seeckt's view that "Poland's existence is unbearable .... It must disappear .... Russia and Germany must re-establish the frontiers of 1914." [1]

During the inter-war years, the Polish government's foreign policy was the "Doctrine of the Two Enemies," which attempted to maintain equilibrium between Germany and the Soviet Union. When Hitler came to power and Germany became increasingly agressive, the Polish government signed treaties and non-aggression pacts and spent so much money on armaments that by the middle of the 1930s half the country's budget went for defense. But Germany and the Soviet Union signed a secret protocol to dismember Poland once again.

On August 22, 1939, Hitler said to his generals, "The destruction of Poland has priority ... . I shall give a propagandist reason for staging the war, no matter whether it is plausible or not. The victor will not be asked afterwards whether he told the truth or not. When starting and waging war it is not right that matters for victory." Hitler finished, "Close your hearts to pity."[2] The Germans fabricated a *casus belli*, including false newsreels of Polish atrocities against the Germans. On September 1, 1939, German troops, accompanied by three SS regiments, marched into Poland, while the Soviets invaded and took their agreed-on half on September 17th.

Poland's Foreign Minister, Josef Beck, was the first in Europe to stand up to Hitler, believing the Germans would withdraw if faced down. He was overly confident about Poland's military preparedness, and believed German military power was exaggerated.

While *Blitzkrieg*, which means "lightning war," is a German word, it was not known to the German army before 1939, and was invented by Western newspapermen to convey an idea of the speed and devastation of the German invasion in the three-week campaign against the poorly equipped Polish army.

Polish Contributions to the War

Polish soldiers valiantly resisted the invasions by Germany and the Soviet Union in 1939. They held off the Germans longer than leaders of other countries thought they could, but the onslaught was too much. Though many Polish soldiers were taken prisoner, others escaped to France where a Government-in-Exile was set up and two divisions were formed which fought with the French Army against the Germans. Polish pilots served in France and, after France capitulated on June 22, 1940, served in England with the Royal Air Force in the Battle of Britain (July 1940-June 1941). Those unable to get out of France formed resistance units. Three Polish destroyers and two Polish submarines were sent to join the Royal Navy. The Podhale Brigade, a mountain troop established in France, served with the Allies at Narvik in Norway; the Carpathian Brigade, organised in Syria, joined the British Forces and fought in Africa. Many Polish soldiers fought in the Red Army, as well as in a separate Polish Army in the Soviet Union. Poles made their way to England from all over the world, regrouped, and fought in France, Belgium, Holland and Germany.

When the Soviets invaded Poland, they took huge numbers of Polish soldiers as prisoners. Some survived, and the release of these men was arranged for by General Sikorski (Premier of the Polish Government-in-Exile). In September 1942, almost 75,000 Poles were let out through Iran, becoming the 2nd Polish Army Corps. Under General Wladyslaw Anders, they fought in Italy from November 1943 on to the end.

The Poles had an effective and courageous underground – there were no Polish Quislings – called the Home Army, led by General Tadeusz Bor-Komoroski. In the fall of 1944 the Home Army in Warsaw led an uprising against the Germans, encouraged to do so by the Soviet Union, which then halted their advance towards the city and let the Poles be slaughtered. Stalin ordered this because he wanted Polish leadership exterminated, and around 200,000 were killed.

Another remarkable contribution of the Poles to the Allies was "Ultra," which was not made public until more than thirty years after the war. In the late 1930s Polish military intelligence along with a group of Polish mathematicians located and built a replica of the German code machine "Enigma." As part of their contribution to the war, the Poles gave their findings to the British, who finished the job of cracking the Enigma codes that the Poles began, enabling the Allies to read Nazi radio signals throughout the war. (Other decrypting done by the British was combined with Enigma, forming "Ultra.")

The condition of Poles under the German occupation was unspeakably horrible. While it is well known that Nazi ideology considered Jews an element to be eliminated from the earth, it is not as well known that they considered Slavs to be subhuman, fit only to be slaves or eliminated. Millions of people were killed in Poland, and by 1945, Poland had lost one-fifth of its prewar population and at least 90 percent of its Jews. Proportionate to its population, Poland lost more people than any other country, and half its wealth was stolen by the Nazis. Poland believed that the Allies would recognize their immense efforts to help defeat Germany, as well as the hardships they had endured, but after the war against the Germans was over, Poland was once again betrayed and was relinquished to the Soviet Union, the other hated oppressor, not to be free again for decades.

Multi-National Poland and the Jews

The Polish government during the 1920s and 1930s was disorganized and confused partly because it was a new country, and partly because the three different sections (formerly under Austria, Prussia, and Russia) of the new Poland had had over one hundred years to develop in three very different ways. In addition, Poland had always been a multi-national state, and about one-third of its population of about twenty-seven million was made up of minorities: Ukrainians, Belorussians, Germans, Russians, Czechs, Lithuanians, while ten percent were Jews.

There were more Jews in Poland than in any other country because Polish kings had welcomed them since at least the thirteenth century. They had come to Poland not only for new economic opportunities, but also to escape persecution in German areas and other countries. Jews were regularly massacred, particularly during plagues (for which they were blamed), and were persecuted for what the Christians said was their part in Christ's death. As a result, the vast majority of Jews in the world lived in Poland, where they had privileges because the kings felt they were necessary to the economy of the country. During the Protestant Reformations in the sixteenth century, when both Protestant and Catholic monarchs were slaughtering those of the other faith, Polish kings had allowed people to worship as they chose, and Poland continued to be an unusually tolerant country.

But the increasing nationalism in the nineteenth century took its toll of Polish tolerance. By the end of the First World War Jews had been so badly mistreated by the Poles that the Allies insisted on a Minorities Treaty for each of the many new countries created or resurrected from the territorial debris of the collapse of the three Empires. This Treaty gave rights to the minor nationalities and allowed the Western Powers to observe adherence to the rules. The Polish people found this an unfair imposition and bitterly resented the Jews for their part in creating the Treaty, while the Jews believed in the Treaty and their new rights. Poles viewed themselves as the native population, and saw Jews as interlopers, as foreigners and strangers.

So long as Marshall Joseph Pilsudski (1867-1935) was alive, Jews were relatively safe, since he was a firm believer in Poland as a multi-cultural state and was not anti-Semitic. His military successes made him a national hero. Unsatisfied with the somewhat inept government, in 1926 he led a military coup, and his government lasted until his death. But after that anti-Semitism grew and there were hundreds of attacks on Jews. Pilsudski had believed in an inclusive Poland in which all of the many minorities would have equal citizenship; Roman Dmowski, the leader of the Endecja Party which became the strongest and encouraged by what was happening in Germany under the Nazis, took steps to exclude Jews from all parts of society, especially economic.

After the war was won, some Jews returned to Poland to look for their families, most of whom had perished. For the most part, the returning Jews were rejected by the Polish survivors.[3] A further burst of extreme anti-Semitism in 1968 forced out the majority of those who remained. Where there had been almost three and a half million Jews and a rich and ancient Jewish culture, there are now something over five thousand, mostly very elderly.

CHAPTER I

I am born in Pulawy

"You've seen in Pulawy Jewish everything."

I was born in Pulawy[4] on 10th September, 1920, on Lubelska Street, 4. Our house had two and a half rooms, used for everything. No bath, we washed in a tub, on Fridays we went to a public bath. We had a toilet–outside, air-conditioned! I had two brothers and three sisters. Noah, the eldest–he was about twelve, thirteen years older than me–was a tailor. He taught himself everything, French, English, Hebrew. Rachel was next, became a dressmaker, then Pearl, who went to Warsaw, worked in the fur business, married Berel Kahn, he worked in a fur store in Warsaw. Mine other brother Scholem–he was two years older than me–was a tailor, too. Cyna, mine youngest sister, younger than me–she was the baby–was in school.

Mine mother's name was Sarah. Mine father's name was Yehudah, called "Yidl" in Yiddish, and he used to make candles and soap so the kids called him Yiddlelechsia. (In every small town there was somebody who made candles from cattle fat and that person was called "Lechsia" *[candlemaker in Yiddish]*) Mine mother and father were very religious. All the kids obeyed the rules and we had very big respect for our parents.

Mine father came from a small town near Pulawy. He had two brothers–one brother, mine uncle David, was in France, the other, mine uncle Gadale, was a teacher in a cheder *(Hebrew school)* in Pulawy. Mine mother's family were from all over, Warsaw, Lublin. Mine mother had three sisters, Pearl, Bluma, and Zelda, and three brothers, Michel, Abram, and Schabsa. Nobody from mine family survived, only mine brother Noah–because he went to Israel around 1935–and a young cousin, second, maybe third cousin–Sara Friedman–survived in Israel but I lost contact with her. I tried after but couldn't find.

It wasn't a rich home, but there was always a piece of fish Friday night, some challah *(egg-glazed holiday bread)* made, maybe some chicken. You didn't see in a whole week meat at all hardly, it was very expensive, but we managed, the whole family had something to eat, mine father made enough for food. We had our own place, we didn't have to pay taxes so much in the house *then*–it got bad later–just a little bit, and you had to have insurance for fire, and that's all. It was a hard life, but the people were nice, polite, very big respect for older people, for stranger people. We didn't need the charity from the Jews in the United States–the American Joint Distribution Committee sent money, they helped Jewish people with food, send money to fix a synagogue, look after a cemetery. They did a lot. Mine father had to be on the Board to give charity, he helped distribute the money, mine family didn't need it.

Mine mother—they find out after—died of gall bladder inflammation in, I think, 1933. She died in Warsaw; they took her from Pulawy. I was still there. Mine uncle Teitelbaum—his wife and mine mother were sisters—he had helped out a boy, Dr. Goldkorn, to become a doctor. (When this boy was studying his father used to beat the boy up—the father was a drunk. Mine uncle paid for his university education.) In Warsaw mine uncle called him, he needed him in the middle of the night. He said, "Listen, you have to go to Pulawy with the ambulance and bring her to Warsaw." A hundred and twenty kilometres. But she died. A young woman. Very religious. Afterwards, mine uncle didn't survive, the doctor didn't survive, nobody survived.

There was only one Jewish girl left in mine home town after the war. I think her name was Topcha Gold. Her family was very well-to-do, they had a big store for groceries, I remember it like now. A boy who was in the Polish Army, he fell in love with her when I was there, in mine boyhood I think she was going out with him. It was a secret, nobody knew nothing—he wasn't Jewish. He saved her during the war and they married and had some children, but she died after. Very little was left of Pulawy, some buildings left, but it's a brand new city. Today lives there sixty thousand people—when I was there it was six thousand!

Pulawy was about half Jewish. Saturday everything was closed in our home town, you didn't see nobody. Gentile people knew that Friday afternoon, it's finished, and they knew when is a Jewish holiday coming, nobody would come to a market or nothing, everything was shut up. You've seen there Jewish everything, Jewish cattle dealers, you've seen Jewish people who went around special to put on windows—some farmers built new homes and need windows, they used to come around, had a special wagon, take out the windows and put the new ones in. There was shoemakers—one man who had about twenty shoemakers working for him, you couldn't wear out the shoes you bought from his place and he used to supply all over.

Two of mine mother's brothers have been in the horse business. (Jews ran the horse business in Poland in those days.) One, mine uncle Schabsa, the youngest one, used to go to a market to buy horses for the beer companies—they wanted to have the same size of horses and they give you a contract, you bring us this size, this colour horses. He had all kinds of horses. He used to sell some and buy other ones, had a stable where he kept thirty-six or forty horses. Mine uncle had seen the Lone Ranger in the movies so he had himself a white horse with black legs, and he trained that horse so that when mine uncle whistled special way to him he stand up on his two back legs.

One year mine uncle went in somewhere and some gypsies stole that white horse. He was a registered horse, and mine uncle had a book of his registered horses. Quite a few months pass, mine uncle and I are out together, came a "tabor" (Polish word, means gypsies one after another, with caravans—they lived like that) and there was a horse caught mine uncle's eye. He said to me, "Wait, Chaimkeleh *(a diminutive for Chaim)*, I'm going to whistle at that horse and you'll see he will stand up on his hind feet." And so he started to whistle, and that horse really knew his own owner! he stood up on the back legs! Mine uncle went down to the gypsy and says, "That's mine horse." The gypsy says, "Can't be." Mine uncle says, "This horse is painted." (The gypsies had painted blond around on the black, on the legs, make it look all white.) The police came, they took turpentine and started washing the horse up and the paint came off. Mine uncle had his book of horses and the police arrested the gypsies, and they give mine uncle back the horse. (Mine uncle Schabsa didn't survive, none of mine mother's family survived.)

I went to public school. I took mine lunch, but before I came to school I eat up the lunch, so I sit hungry all day in school! (Breakfast was two slices of bread with marmalade and some tea, wasn't enough for me.) Later the ladies' auxiliary made that, rich and poor, if the children want at 11:30-12:00 they could have the milk and rolls the ladies used to bring–you have your own cup–and they give it to you free. The kids from well-to-do families didn't want, but I was always waiting to get a double portion! I was always hungry!

Mostly Jewish kids went to that school, they taught Jewish religion. Some teachers were Polish, and my favourite one was Mrs. Szeprawska, the youngest one, a beautiful young woman. She taught sports–soccer was our favourite sport, and I was good–during school we had exercise and we played then. After if you wanted to go higher than Grade 7 you had to pay, you have to have a lot of money–we were poor–not *very* poor, but poor. I was fourteen when I finished school.

We didn't go Saturday to school–Saturday and Sunday we didn't go–but then the government passed a law that all the Jewish kids should go Saturday to school, too. That was when I was finishing public school. Mine youngest sister Cyna went on Saturdays but she didn't have to write or anything, just to listen to the lessons.

Every day after school I went to cheder–to Hebrew school. I had an uncle, Gadale Goldberg, mine father's brother, almost six feet tall, and when he walked on the street, everybody knew him. He taught everything to himself, read a lot, he was a teacher for Hebrew, to write, Jewish, figuring. They had two hundred students. I was bar mitzvahed but they didn't make a fuss–here they make such a fuss like you have never seen! I know, I have ten grandsons! Mine father brought a bottle of schnapps to the synagogue and some cookies and that was all–no big tsimmis *(fuss)*, who could afford that? (To tell you the truth, I'm not sure how he could buy the schnapps even!) I just made a prayer in Hebrew and that's all!

We spoke Yiddish at home, we spoke Polish most of the time at school, German I learned in school, but when Hitler came to power, they quit teaching it. I understood some Russian but didn't have it in school. I learned Lithuanian when I started to work for the fur business, but I forgot most of it after. I didn't know English, I learned here in Canada, and in the army in Scotland.

After we started getting bigger, mine oldest brother Noah was away in the army, mine next sister Rachel was a dressmaker–she used to design dresses, if you want she'll show you dresses in a book, she'll make for you. Mine sister Pearl worked in a fur place in Warsaw, and Cyna, the next sister, the baby, was in school. Mine other brother Scholem went to learn the trade of a tailor, too, like Noah. If you didn't have education, you had to become a tradesman, and that's it. They have worked hard. Good times, bad times. What could you do? But to make a living wasn't so hard–you didn't need a telephone, you didn't need a car.

Then the government pressed the taxes so much, mine father closed up his shop making soap and candles, next to the house. (It stinked from half a mile from that fat for soap!) After he closed up we used to deliver to the boats special fat. Mine father used to melt this fat from the cattle–you couldn't have any particles, if not clean, it would eat up the motors–and he used to sell quite a bit of it. The boats took the fat with them and mixed it with oil. This didn't stink, very pure stuff, couldn't keep it too long.

I didn't have a bicycle. Mine neighbour, his name was Boimal–they had six boys, no girls. He was a big buyer from lumber, came from Hamburg, very well-to-do, and they had a brand new bicycle with balloon tires. I said, "How about lending me your bike?" and he said, "Chaimke, take it, we got three in the house." I used to take it and go for a ride–I used to enjoy it so much! But I couldn't afford it, a bicycle was a luxury. (I find out after that before the war here in North America was also bad. We had a cousin in New York, he was a writer in the *Forwarts*–the Jewish newspaper–and he send a letter in Depression time that a man is waiting for another man to drop a cigarette butt on the street so he'll have a smoke!)

We had quite a few boys going swimming, in the Vistula River. Girls, too. Mine brother was a good swimmer. (We had an uncle in France, used to swim and play the violin and never make it wet. This I had from mine brother, I didn't know mine uncle. When I was in the army I went to see him when I came to France right after it was liberated. I brought some food, took a friend who knew French, and went with a jeep down there where I thought he was living. I knocked on the door but the house was blocked up and the French people told mine friend that the Germans took him. They said, "There's one daughter who survived and she lives on the street where the Eiffel Tower is." They give the address and we went but the woman said, "No, that's not me." I never heard, never find out.)

We lived near the Vistula and some cousins of ours had some wooden rowing boats. When I was a little bit older I asked them if I could have one of the boats. There were well-to-do Jewish people in mine home town who in the summer evenings liked to go take a swim–they didn't really swim, they'd rush around in the water–and a lot of boys didn't want to take them, they didn't want to row. I used to take people on the boat and wash them around–rubbed them around with some soap–and bring them back. Saturday we had people come early in the morning before they went to synagogue and they came there to wash. People wanted to cool off in the summer. Every day–summertime, vacation time. I did a good job, I was the favourite one to do this! Every one would give me a zloty—you could buy a lot of stuff for that—sometimes I had four, five passengers. I enjoyed that. So I always had a few pennies—we called them groschen—in mine pocket, but I give most to mine mother.

In summertime people used to take lumber from the Tatar Mountains around Crakow, by water on the Vistula, and they used to go to Gdansk—it was cheap with the water to take the lumber. Mr. Boimal was in that line of business, used to cut the lumbers and ship them out—and they had special men who lived on those logs, they make a shack on them. When they came to a bridge they had to hold the lumber so it wouldn't hit the bridge, used to put pieces of wood to keep it from going so fast. We used to row in the little boats—quite a few people, not me alone, but other ones—and we bought the wood pieces that was no good for them—too short. We give them some tobacco. I used to bring the wood, four or five pieces, tie them down in back in the water, dragged behind, and bring them home. We dried them up and mine grandfather—may he rest in peace—cut them up in pieces, and we had wood for the winter.

Mine father's father, Abram Yitzak, lived in our house after mine grandmother died. Mine mother treat him like gold, he was a nice man. Before he passed away—it was the 18th of July, it was a hot day—he went to a steam bath, he drinked the whole siphon of cold water, and he got sick the next day, he catched pneumonia. He was laying sick for six days in the house. He said to call up the head man who looked after the dead people. He told him—I remember like now, the man's name was Wolf—"Listen, Wolf, tomorrow's going to be a hot day," and mine Zeyde *(grandfather in Yiddish)* opened up a little door in his dresser. He had there a few zloty, a couple bottles of schnapps (95% spirit! strong stuff!), to go for the people who washed him (before they bury Jewish people they have to wash them), and says, "Get ready, I don't want to lay around here too long." Mine father said a prayer, mine grandfather lifted up his hands, said a prayer, closed his eyes. About six o'clock in the morning he passed away and by ten o'clock he was already in the cemetery. He was 86 years old. I watched all this.

Chapter II

I go to Warsaw

Mine sister Pearl said, "You'll learn something."

I finished school in 1934, I went away to Warsaw, I went to learn a trade in the fur business, wholesale. (Otto Preminger's brother owned our place, Simon Preminger–he got away, went to Israel with his wife, his kids went to England. When I was stationed there I used to see them, take them food, clothes, during the war.) I got the job through Pearl. Mine sister said, "You'll learn something." The store was called Polsky Zjednoczony Przemyst Kuszniersky (Polish United Fur Company) on Bielanska 18. It was a wholesale company for sheepskin linings for jackets, coats. Also in our business we made a lot for the government–the Air Force need jackets, we made for them, if they need for the railroad special warm coats, we made for them, for the army we made. You know, we had big contracts.

I lived in the fur store, had mine own room, a washroom, mine clothes, could make a cup of tea. I ate mine meals in a restaurant. I took messages, and opened up in the morning. Early in the morning a lot of religious people–they came to buy fur from all over Poland–came in our store to say their prayers–the train arrived early and they didn't have where to go. They treated me like gold, those people.

Mine sister worked in a big fur place, retail, for our uncle Teitelbaum–she was managing the uncle's store on account he had asthma from fur, had to give him needles to breathe. Her husband Berel Kahn worked in a big fur place next door to her. (Berel was in the army when the Russians took half of Poland–he was a prisoner-of-war in Russia–in Siberia. He was released 1941– Sikorski made a pact with Stalin the Polish soldiers can go out from Russia. He survived, he came back, the war was over, mine sister was dead from the Germans, it was no good for Jews in Poland. He came to Israel, he had to go to the army, he married again but his wife was always sick. He was such a nice boy. I met him in Israel, I give him some pictures of Pearl.)

Pearl ran the whole business. I said to mineself, "If ever mine uncle wants to sell I would like to be a shareholder." He had a very good name in the business. Whenever I had a few extra zlotys I put in a savings account and I said, "Look, Pearl, if ever you and your husband decided to go for yourself and uncle wants to sell the business, you'll buy it and I'll be a partner." Where I worked we had special pieced linings for men's coats, made from sheepskin. The sheepskin was cut for inside linings, then go to a special place where they make them softer–soaked in water and chemicals, make soft leather from hard leather. I used to call mine sister, "Listen, Pearl, you come down to our place, we got six boxes of sewed-together linings, ask uncle if he wants to buy." He used to go with her, he looked and give a cheque to mine boss, and they made money on that, depending on the quality–there was a big markup, the demand was very big. They put pieces together to match, but sometimes they didn't match, and they just hurry up to get rid of it. They worked hard, but they made a nice living.

The only thing they had troubles with was in a Sunday you couldn't keep open a store[5], they had to watch for the police. They couldn't keep open, but they went inside to show something, and somebody stayed outside to watch and that's all, or you had to pay a fine. The laws said you had to be closed on Sunday, it was a day of rest for everybody, including Jewish people. Everybody had to keep closed, the only time you could keep open a store on Sunday was before a holiday, before a Christmas, a New Year's, a Easter–people wanted to buy, so you could open it up twelve o'clock and keep it open until six. Where I worked in that big company it was open Saturday, the gentile boys came to work Saturdays to deal with customers, Jewish boys worked on Sundays inside, checked things, marked things down. (Sometimes on Sunday I went to see a soccer game, I give another boy 4-5 zlotys to do my work so I could go.)

But the Polish government had already started to pass laws against Jews.[6] They came out with signs in the stores, "Don't buy from a Jew." Hitler being in Germany brought in so much more propaganda. The whole fur business stayed in Jewish hands in Poland and when some big Polish stores (as elegant as Fifth Avenue in New York) came to buy from us–the Jewish dealers in fur–the big wholesalers made up their minds not to sell to them. They said, "You coming to buy from us, and you put on signs in your windows you shouldn't buy from a Jew the merchandise!" They said, "You're taking the sign off or if not we are going to organize that we are not going to sell you nothing, nobody, we're not going to stay in the business." So they started taking the signs off in some of the big stores, but they stayed on other ones all over Poland, they came more and more these signs. They got rid of Jews where they could, all over, from all kinds businesses, they changed things just to get rid of them. It got very hard for Jews to make a living.

The Falanga[7]–Polish Fascists–listened to Hitler, they hated Jews, they got money from Hitler. When Pilsudski was there, he held anti-Semitism down in the government, in the country–he didn't believe in it–but when he died–May 12th in 1935, I remember like now–and Smigley-Ridz became head man it was starting to get bad, worser and worser. They had a pogrom in June in Grodno after Pilsudski died–they didn't have any since maybe 1920–and later another one in another place. When Pilsudski was alive, a lot of Jewish boys went into the army, served in the army, were brilliant soldiers, were officers. When Smigley-Ridz took over it was altogether different, Jewish boys weren't promoted, it was very hard.

In the university Jewish students had to sit on the ghetto benches–they made them sit separate in the classroom on these–so a lot of them stood up all through their years.[8] Never sat down! got into trouble for that, they got beat up by Polish students. The Falanga didn't want any Jews to be educated–they were like Hitler.

Anti-Semitism kept increasing every day, every day. In the Polish Government, in the Senate, there used to be a woman, Pristalova, the first thing she brought up that the Jews shouldn't be able to kill and kosher any cattle.[9] Pilsudski–our big man–he said, "Did you already see if the army has everything, you have nothing to think about, this is laying in your mind?" He was a liberal man. It was getting more and more against Jews, the government worked against Jews, people started closing up their businesses. We have seen they have started sending Jews from Germany–take nothing with them, they have stripped them of everything, they have had Kristallnacht. Things were very bad.

And in mine country, in Poland, the government didn't see that we need this, we need that. People didn't have in Poland for themselves sugar but they sent out bags for 10 cents–10 groschen–a kilo to England. They made material in Lodz–there was a factory for white linen there, material for suits, for everything. The British came along–they made the linen over there in Poland on account labour was cheap and they put on a stamp, "Produce of England," not produce of Poland, and that's how everything went that way for export. Lumber! The nicest furniture went to England, Scotland, came from Poland, went over there. Pork! they sold all kinds of hams, everything pork in cans, and our Polish people didn't have. (I didn't eat, but Polish people ate.) In the army, what did you get? For ten days eighty-five cents–eighty-five groschen, wasn't even a zloty. It was very hard.

CHAPTER III

The Germans Invade Poland

"I figured I'd come back but it never happened."

The Germans came into Poland, September 1, 1939–very early in the morning, no warning, no declaring war, just soldiers and bombs everywhere. (Later they called it blitzkrieg, the Germans invented this for Poland.) On September 6th, in Warsaw, they announced on the radio anybody who can hold a weapon and is over seventeen years of age, to cross the Vistula River, any place over there because they were forming the army, so I left for there. I wasn't fit yet to be a soldier, I hadn't had any training. (I was registered already when I was eighteen but you didn't get called up till you were nineteen.) I wanted to serve in the Polish Army but the announcement was a fake, the Germans got in with that news to make trouble. You couldn't tell what was what, all kinds of stories on the radio, what was going on we couldn't know.[10] (I heard after the Germans said we started the war, we attacked them, but they always told lies about Poland. *They started.*)

The Polish government and some soldiers got out from Warsaw, went through Rumania, went to France, have a Polish government there. (After the government was in England, after France give up to the Germans.) For me that way was not good, it was too far from Warsaw–those soldiers have been close to the border and I wasn't a soldier, I was a civilian. I said good-bye to Pearl–she didn't want to go with me, Berel went away to the army, she wanted to wait there. I didn't go home to see mine father, never went anywhere, didn't see nobody. When I left on the sixth day I figured I'd come back soon but it never happened. We went just where we could reach the best destination, the shortest. We have been going just anyplace–I wasn't dreaming of Vilna, I figured just get out of Warsaw and then come back. People figured the Germans would be defeated but I think, "It's impossible to defeat Germany, they have too much." We figured the German Army would come in and *behave like an army.* People didn't think, didn't believe the Germans would start up killing Jewish people left and right and Polish people left and right, take them away in slave labour to Germany, burn up villages. We started to go any place, go wherever you could go.

I took a little bit clothes, and we walked to Szedlec, about sixty kilometres from Warsaw, and when we came to that place the Germans started to bomb the hell out of us, the Germans bombed our highways, hundreds of people have been laying dead. I went with mine manager from the fur business (his name was Tulek Argend) and with some cousins of mine who worked with me in the shop (Leo, Benjamin, and Isaac Teitelbaum). The Germans started to bomb so bad we couldn't go back, we had to keep moving on.

I bought from a man a horse and wagon, and we went on, and later we got into the woods and we give the horse a rest and a man from Szedlec said to us, "The Germans are here, not far away–you can hear the tanks." I said, "You look after the horse, mister," and I took off one way, mine director from the business he went with me, and mine three cousins went another way and we lost them in the woods. We went in different directions. And that's all. I never saw them again, they didn't survive, nobody survived.

Mine director and I, we went over a field–wherever it was–and we reached Szedlec and we stayed there. (Szedlec was a small town, full with refugees, from all over. Never been there before, stayed there a few hours, wasn't a place where I could even lay down outside on the grass there were so many people, couldn't buy any food, nothing.) That was before the Jewish High Holidays–September 14th was New Year's in that year, in 1939. That night we heard that the Russians are giving up all that territory and the Germans are taking it over.

Near Szedlec there was Bialapodlaska which the Germans bombed out–it used to be a Polish Air Force station, air port and everything, and they bombed the hell out of that, everything was on fire. I said, "I'm not going to stay here, I'm going to go." Mine director said, "We have to keep moving, we'll go, that's all." One Jewish family took us in for lunch–lunch was a piece of dark bread, I remember like now, and they had some apples–and then we left, we came down towards the Bug River.

The Russians came in Poland 17th September–like the Germans, they didn't say they're going to do it–and Germany and Russia divided, took for themselves all of Poland. I was afraid the Germans would start picking us up to forced labour, as they have done in Warsaw–picking up people by the thousands–so I decided to go to the Russian side. (There was no fighting–the Russians came from one side, the Germans from the other, they took what they wanted, divided Poland in half.)

The Germans didn't bother to stop us, we came to the Russian side and the Russian soldier was saying right away with the bayonet, "Where are you going?" We told him we lived not far away from here, "We're going home," and he said, "Let me tell you something, Tovarich," he said, "Comrade, you are going to live in our country but you will forget about making love." It was funny–comes out good in Russian! (I speak just a little bit, I never went to school for Russian language.)

We came back to Szedlec, and we looked around and Russians and Germans didn't exactly make up their mind where the borders are going to be–some people said the Vistula River, but after they changed their mind and chose the Bug River. The Germans stayed over there, and we asked them in the German language, "Can you go out from Warsaw, can you go into Warsaw?" "Yes, you can go in and go out." (I would go back but I was afraid, some people said as soon as you go they take you for slave labour.) We decide maybe Vilna, we knew people there, so we asked the Germans, and they said, "You have till tonight, you can go in or you can go out, and the Bug River is going to be the border."

We went across the Bug again, and the Russians have been there. They ask me where I am going and I said, "I live here," and they let me go. In the evening, back in Szedlec, we finally make up our minds. I said, "Mr. Argend, what are you going to do? We walk, we are going to fall into prison to the Germans. We can try to go to Bialystok, from Szedlec to Bialystok isn't so far." Mr. Argend said, "Chaim, I would like to go back to Warsaw, to mine wife and mine boy. I'll go from Bialystok." (You could go out from Bialystok, not from other places.) We went into the market to try what we could, and we have seen a Russian truck with soldiers–the commander of the truck is unloading the soldiers there. We asked the commander if he'd take us–Mr. Argend give him a watch (I had one too but I held on to it for after–the commander only wanted one watch.) He took us in the truck and when we came on the road, Russian guards asked him what he has and he said, "I only got ammunition, and the ammunition is sealed." And he took us down to Bialystok.

We came and stayed with a family Trafimofsky–I knew him from before, from the fur business–he took us in the house and give us a place to sleep on the floor and something to eat. It was very bad there. I told mine friend Mr. Argend, "Listen, I am not going to stay here, there's too many refugees"–there were thousands and thousands in Bialystok–"there's no place where to rent, what to eat. I've decided, I'm going to Vilna." And he said, "I'll tell you, Chaim, if you're going to Vilna, I'll give you a letter." Mine company had a very big store from fur there, and a lady, Mrs. Salit, used to run it. I begged him not to go back to Warsaw. I said, "Listen, come with me," but he went back to save his wife and boy. A very nice man. (He didn't survive. He went back to Warsaw, they had already taken his wife away to a camp, and an SS man came to take away him and his little boy–good-looking boy–and when that SS man took that boy, Mr. Argend took out a bottle and shoved it right in his face, and that SS man shot him and he shot that little boy. Shot them both. This is what I found out after, how he finished his life. I never told his wife. Just after the war was over, I was still in the Polish Army and I went to Bergen-Belsen[11]–the British liberated it–and I saw her and her sister–they didn't recognize me. Next day I took them clothes, I took down some food for them, and she give me her brother's address in Chicago. I wrote and he made out papers to bring them to the United States and I've never seen them again.)

In Bialystok, I took a train–it was free–the Russians made the trains go as they had a lot of things to transport. There's no glass in the windows, all damaged from the bombs, artillery, from airforce, nobody stopped them–they did anything they wanted–but the train is going to Vilna. I was really hungry, and I had cigarettes with me–cigarettes were a monopoly of the Polish government which opened up their stores and give away cigarettes because who would collect the money? I never smoked but I took 400. I give a soldier a hundred cigarettes (I remember like now, it was Unake brand!) and he give me a loaf of bread. I fell asleep in that train and somebody stole mine bread! But that was nothing, you know.

Chapter IV

I go to Vilna

"Whatever the Russians wanted, they took, whatever they wanted to take, they did, and where it went nobody knows."

I came to Vilna, it was the end of September, the Jewish Holidays have been almost over, 1939.[12] I was nineteen. Lithuania was a free country but didn't have Vilna, the Allies give it over to Poland in 1920. Now the Russians took Vilna from Poland, give it over to Lithuania–not just the city, the whole district. They said, "That's yours. It's a gift from Stalin!" That was in October. (After, the Russians took over Vilna and Lithuania and Latvia, Estonia, everything. And when the Russians came in a city–they occupied–they made all kinds of movies, in parks, boys and girls have been dancing in the street, *all smiling.* All propaganda.)

There have been a lot of Polish soldiers headed home to Vilna and the Russians wanted to take them to prison. They started to take Polish soldiers to prison just like that! (The Russians have been afraid the Poles would fight them, like before.) I saw two soldiers in uniform and one soldier said, "Can you give me that coat, mister?" (I had a brand-new coat on.) "Cover mine uniform? I want to get in a droshka"–that's a closed-in horse and buggy. The Russians were around all over. He put on mine coat, got in the droshka and handed the coat back through the window to me. Then I give the other one the coat and the two of them got away, and I got mine coat back. I met them after–two boys from Vilna–one day on the street.

When I came to Vilna, I didn't have where to go, so I went down to the big wholesale fur market–maybe I meet somebody I've seen before. People have been coming from all over the world and they bought and sold fur there. The biggest fur market in the world has been in Leipzig, Germany. But now–since the fur business has been in Jewish hands, they didn't buy fur there after Hitler–they made the big fur market in Vilna. Big wholesalers used to come and see the fur and mark down what they want–they had samples sitting around–and they used to ship them. I've been in Vilna a few months before for mine boss, in June and July the same year.

I went down to a hotel where I had stayed before and the owner said, "Chaimke, I haven't got any room but I can give you blankets, you can sleep here in the corridor, everything is taken." I said, "Can you let me have a bath?" and he said, "Go ahead." So I stayed there. I had a couple shirts with me and I changed mine clothes. And at night I went downtown.

It was a holiday, Succoth *(Feast of Tabernacles, a harvest festival),* and the Russians had a very big concert. I said to mineself, "I'm going to go, I haven't got what to do, I'll go down." I saw there a man named Abrasher–this is Abraham in Lithuanian-Jewish–Schmerkovicz. I met him before when I was in Vilna on mine boss's business, and his father and his sister-in-law and his wife. At the concert he has seen me and he called me over and said, "Where are you staying at?" I said, "I'm staying in this-and-this hotel, there's no room but I sleep any place I can. The man said he's going to give me a room free on account the Russians are going to take over the hotel." He said, "I'll tell you what, we'll make room in our flat. Take your belongings and you come to our house and stay with us." There was him, his wife, their baby, her mother and father, and the wife's two sisters, Fonia Wellis, about twenty, and the other was Ruchaleh, about seventeen. They wouldn't let me go, I had to go move in over there, in that house, Rudnicka 12, near the big church. I was just like a son to them. I stayed till the last day I left Vilna. To make a living I worked in Mr. Schmerkovicz's nickel-galvanizing factory. I used to buff the samovars, spoons, old ones, and forks, they were silver-plated and we put on new silver.

(The Schmerkovicz family: somebody's alive and I can't trace them. I told mine niece in Israel to put a notice in the paper, the *Jerusalem Post,* and in Hebrew papers, but nobody answered.

But there was here in Windsor one lady, she was telling me she have seen, she spoke to the girls from that family. But she didn't have an address, didn't have nothing. I couldn't ever find.)

I have seen the Russian Army come in to occupy Lithuania and the way they have been dressed!–very poor dress. The soldiers had a coat and here at the bottom, the hem, it was not finished, everything was hanging out from him. (I can show you pictures of us in the Polish Army, how nice and clean. I feel sorry for them Russian boys, how they lived: horses have been pulling their kitchens, food they cooked while the horses have been pulling it. The Russians have been behind years and years and years, you know. In mine time in the Polish Army in Europe, we stopped, and they put on food in the truck, cooked on gas, and we stopped for so long on the road, and after, you finished, and away we go, but we've never been hungry.)

The Russian soldiers carried around a lot of money, Russian rubles, but people didn't want to take it, there was nothing to be bought for that. The Russian closed up the stores, only in the market could you buy anything. The best seller in the market was a small watch.[13] The Russian soldiers used to come in the market–and what they liked to buy is a watch, that was *something* to bring back for his girlfriend or somebody, a watch. Heh! A boy in the market showed them a big watch, and the soldier said he wanted a small one, and the boy told him, "You can make two small ones from the big one," and he bought it–this was not a joke! Some of the watches didn't work even, but if it ticked in the back, they bought it, they carried it around, fifty rubles, a hundred rubles. If you would see how they were fooled! the people sold them a nightgown, not one but hundreds of them, for a Russian lady to dress up with, a nightgown! to go to the opera or restaurant or something.

When the Russian commander came in Vilna–he was a Jew–he wanted to say a prayer for his parents who died, for the memorial service to the year. He came into the oldest synagogue–the Great Synagogue–in Vilna on Niemiecka Ulica (German Street they called it). He asked the man who looks after the synagogue, "Can I say the prayers here?" and he said, "If you know, go ahead." And he said very good his prayers and when he finished the service, the people start asking him questions. One asked him, "Do you have lemons in Russia?" He said, "We got a zavot–a factory–for lemons." Another asked, "Do you have oranges?" "We got a factory for oranges," "We got a factory for matches." They asked, "Do you have poverty in your country?" and he said, "Everything is in our country! Poverty is in our country and it's coming to your country too!" I was there and I have seen it with mine own eyes.[14]

The Russians were starting to liquidate everything, all the shops. If there's no owners they came right away and took, if there's owners they had to show the books, the money, the stock, etc. They came in with revolvers–"Show us the books!" They send in first a man to take stock, then confiscated the place, they took everything out, they left the people with nothing–not just Jews, *everybody*. Whatever the Russians wanted, they took, whatever they wanted to take, they did, and where it went nobody knows. They give a receipt–a nothing–and that was the end of it in Vilna. Everybody who had a store tried to get out everything from the store and hide it.

Mine company had a big warehouse full of fur in Vilna, and in Bialystok Mr. Argend said to me, "Look, if the Russians are going to take over the store, take whatever you want." I took the letter Mr. Argend give me and I went away to see that lady, Mrs. Salit, who was running the Vilna branch of our business. (The people who owned it came from Austria–they were Jewish–Warsaw was the main store, and there were three other stores including Vilna.) I said, "Listen, I got a letter here, Mr. Argend said I should get as much stuff as I can, take something before the Russians are coming and take it over." They had already started to sell out everything that they could. I took out a lot of stuff, I loaded up, I grabbed whatever fur I could and hide it in the place where I worked as a nickel galvanizer. I knew it's going to come in handy–better for me than for the Russians! I took Mr. Schmerkowicz and I said, "You come with me, you help me." You couldn't hold it in their house–no room. We hid over there in the factory everything we could–special jackets, big jackets made from sheepskin (called in Polish kozuch) anything you could sell, and whenever I wanted something I sold some fur thing. Mr. Schmerkovicz always wanted to give me some more money but I didn't need. You know why? I used to go up to the market, sell some of that fur I took from the store, and I had money enough for mineself. Later I went into other business, but I kept working in the factory, too.

Mail was going through from Lithuania to Poland so I wrote to mine family. I heard twice from mine father, once he said to me he hasn't got anything, hasn't got what to sell and hasn't got any money, could I send a parcel? I didn't have any money then so I sold my Omega watch. For it I got 53 lit–that's Lithuanian money–and made a parcel and send it–soap, tea, meat, canned goods, twenty pounds, package had to be made of plywood, the mailman sealed it up, they sent it away. This was the last time I heard from mine family. I never got any mail any more, this parcel I don't know if mine father got. But I could write my cousin Chaim Goldberg, who was in Israel, from Lithuania it went if you wrote it not in Jewish, not in Polish but in German language. It went out from Lithuania somehow to Israel (to Palestine), it went from different ways around.

And some owners of big stores on Niemiecka Street, a beautiful street–like Fifth Avenue–Pordminsky, Chonowicz, they came to me, they knew me from before, and said to me, "The Russians are coming to take over mine store in two days. Chaimke, if you like, take whatever you want, take something to sell on the market, if you get enough you'll give me something, if not keep for yourself." So I took out a few suits, a few coats–they had a very big stock, so I took. And after Goldberg (he's not from mine family)–he lived in Strszuna Street–he said, "Chaimke, you come down in our store and take something too." The Russians took everything that was left.

Mr. Schmerkowicz's father-in-law, Mr. Wellis, he had a special agency for rubber boots, galoshes for women, for men, one of the biggest companies in Poland–everything in rubber. (Mr. Wellis looked after one of the big stores in Vilna.) A man sold us cheap–the Russians are going to take away his business–a few hundred pairs of ladies' rubber boots, with zippers, high heels, maybe we could sell them. In the bottom was marked "Made in Leningrad," in the Russian language. And the soldiers couldn't figure out how come. They said, "We can't get in Russia and this is made in Leningrad and you got it here." It was for export, you know.

Feivel Schmerkowicz, a brother of the man I stayed with, he worked for General Electric in Vilna, they used to make samovars, they used to make radios, they used to make teakettles, all kinds of stuff. One day the Russians came and said that anyone who wants to go to Russia they'll give him a wagon and load up the family with everything. This Schmerkowicz–he was a big Communist, a big organizer of them–decided to go, and when he went to Russia he took a lot of young people with him. When they came over the borders the Russians took everybody separate, the kids separate, the women separate, the husbands separate. They investigate them, put some away in jails, some in factories, everybody in different directions. Feivel went to a trial, he got ten years, Urals. You know what they tell him in the court? "You haven't been good for the Polish, you haven't been good for us, we didn't ask you to come here. Communism is in our country, but you didn't make Communism in your country, and we don't need you!"

How did I find out? There was a boy, Chaimke they called him, the father had a tobacco shop, he was not far away from the borders. He have seen what goes on, and he escaped from Russia. He ran off and a farmer told him, "If you will give me your suit I'll give you mine white suit"–you know farmers, what they wear–"and I'll take you over the borders," and that boy came back from Russia and he was telling the story to people, what happened to all them people like that.

Vilna went back and forth, Lithuanians, Russians. The Russians take everything, the Lithuanians have been rotten towards refugees, towards Jews, towards anybody wasn't a Lithuanian. They wouldn't give you the right time on the day! You know the Lithuanians wouldn't allow a refugee to be selling in the market, or working in a place, so I had false documents made that I am born here in Lithuania. Documents–there was some people in Vilna who had been from the Polish government–who had a knowledge how to make the card what you needed to show you lived here, were registered here. And that's it–they didn't bother you no more if you had that card. Not only Jewish boys–gentile boys–we all worked together to live in Vilna, to make a living, to stay in the market. *Everybody* had some sort of false documents. When I left I had to get rid of every paper, teared it up, burned it up, nothing even for a souvenir. Too dangerous!

There were people from Warsaw who turned up in Vilna. One day in January, in 1940, I was standing on a line at the post office to buy some stamps, and I have seen outside a fellow who was walking with a bag from potatoes and all his belongings in it. I asked the lady in front of me, "Please, I'll come right back." I jumped out to the man and that was him, Isaac Ruchleimer, a friend from Pulawy–he was going to school with mine brother in Pulawy. (Isaac Ruchleimer was about twelve years older than me, I knew him in Pulawy, I knew him in Warsaw, we had been friends. He worked in leather, soft leather for ladies' coats, men's jackets, ladies' handbags. He used to like to go see operas, symphony orchestra all the time–he and mine brother used to go special.) He looked at me, I looked at him, we lost our voices complete. He had on a pair torn pants and an old coat, he was cold, it was winter time.

I asked him how come he was dressed like that, "What happened to you, you haven't any clothes?" He said, "I crossed the borders, and the Russians took everything away from me." He said he had gone away from Warsaw, from the Germans, to Lida, in the Russian zone, but he couldn't make a living there, couldn't make a living with the Russians. I asked him when he got to Vilna. He said, "Just now, just today." I said, "Listen, where you going?" He said, "I am going to look around, I have reached a deal with a man with leather and he is supposed to live here on Trotska Street, and maybe they will give me a place to stay for a while till I warm up."

"First of all," I said, "You can't go like that. I got a piece of material, I'll go into that tailor shop, the man will make you a pair of pants and I got a few zlotys and you'll buy a coat." I dressed him up a little bit, and I said, "Take that bag from the potatoes, throw it away, I'll get something else." He said, "That's all that I got, I got three shirts, a few pair of underwear and a pair of socks, and that's what I got for mineself." I bought him what to wear, he found a place with a family on Zawalna Street–he knew the people from before, he did business with these people, and we opened up a business together. We used to go to Kovno, to Shavel, about 120 kilometres from Vilna, by train–everything was working–buy merchandise, bring them back. We rented a gate for a stall from mine house–that's how you sold stuff there–and we used to sell stockings and thread and blouses, anything you want we could find, we could sell. Since the Russians closed up all the stores, only place to buy anything was from stalls, everybody had a stall. And that's how we lived.

(When I was going to Israel the first time to see mine brother I met a man—we had been sitting on the plane, he looked at me and I looked at him. I said, "Didn't you live on Rodistka 12?" and he said, "Yes, I did," and I said, "Didn't you have this-and-this stall for ladies' wear?" "Yeah, it's me," and I said, "I lived in Schmerkowicz's house." "Oh, your name is Chaim!" I can't remember his name now. He had the biggest stall on the street where I lived in Vilna. The Russians came and took people away for no reason and send them away to Siberia, and they took him. I asked him why, and he said, "No reason, they didn't have any records against me or nothing but for no reason they put me away in a jail and that's it." I said, "Did you go on a trial?" "No, I never went on a trial." I asked the stewardess she can sell us a bottle of liquor? and we had a few drinks. We came into Tel Aviv, it was night, dusty, hot, and I came down and I kissed the ground—you know, like the Pope!—you have to make a prayer the first time. I can't believe that I have seen this man, that he has survived!)

Chapter VI

We leave Vilna

"I have seen that time is running out."

Ruchleimer and I had a very good business going but I have seen that the time is running out. I had been there a year. We are making enough money to live, getting by, but money wasn't interesting us: we have seen that war is coming between Germany and Russia. We wanted to get out. It started to get tight, every day, every day we hear the Russians are concentrating troops, the Germans are concentrating troops. Things are not so good for us.

One day I get a letter from the Russian Government to come to register. I'll have to go to the Russian Army! I said, "I am not going to serve Stalin." I was against Communism always at home, so I wouldn't serve in the Russian Army even against Hitler. The man who looked after the apartment house knew everybody who lives there and one day he tells me the man from the registration said to him, "You know what, we got a list here of a lot of them young fellows who're living around here." He said to me, "They are going to draft you into the Russian Army, you know." I said, "Don't mark down nothing, this person doesn't live here any more, and you don't know him."

I talked to mine friends. Ruchleimer and I wanted to go to Estonia and from there to Finland and go away from there but we had tips from some other boys who tried that the borders are too heavy guarded both from the Germans and from the Russians. I talked around to friends, everybody talks of this–stay or go? which? how? We hear the Japanese consul in Kovno give out transit visas to go through Japan, for people who wanted to leave the country.[15] (I later find he gives out visas, even when he was leaving, when the Japanese Government told him to stop, on the train home he was giving out, signing them.) We asked some leaders from Jewish organizations what to do. A man said, "Don't try to get Japanese transit visas–the Russians will arrest you, they'll put you away to Siberia, they've done it to other ones." One day I was down at the train station and I saw that same man with a Japanese visa. I have seen that he is leaving Lithuania–everybody wants for themselves everything!

Mine friend Ruchleimer says, "We'll try." So we went to Kovno to the Japanese Embassy to try to get a visa to go. When we came it was too late, the Embassy was closed up, finished, they stopped them. (This was in September, 1940.) What are we going to do? We had to look around how to get out from Lithuania. So we go find someone who makes false papers–good ones–to make visas for us. Why didn't we take them before? We have been afraid. People have said, "They are going to arrest you, Chaim, or something." Now I said to mineself, "Don't listen to nobody, make up your mind and go!" So we decided we'll make. Somebody will give us a visa and we'll make a stamp, and we'll go.

Abram Richter made us the false papers, and put on special stamps–he was a watchmaker, that was his trade. We give him a thousand lit in Lithuanian money for each visa, ten visas in all–but he give us one free, maybe two. The Japanese visa is hard: we got one from one man, made like a photostat, but this wasn't a photostat, very complicated, but Abram could do it. (I still have a picture of Abram Richter. He's alive, lives in Israel. When I was there, I called a number, got a lady and I said, "Did your husband come from Japan to India? and he married a lady from India?" "Yes, that's mine husband and I'm his wife." "Can you tell your husband that a friend of his is looking for him? I come from Canada, mine name is Chaim Goldberg." He told me, "When I applied to the Red Cross, they said you got killed in Normandy." "It wasn't me, it was the other Goldberg–there were two Goldbergs in mine regiment." When he saw me he started to cry and we sat and ate and talked together many times. You know how Richter survived? He went away like I went to Japan, he went with the Trans-Siberian train, but he decided to go to India. In India he met a girl from a fine Jewish family, Indian Jewish, he married her and after he went to Israel. He served in the Israeli Army three times: in 1967 he was on the battlefield, in other wars he was on the Syrian border. I went with him into a Russian tank the Israelis have taken.)

We had to give these visas to the Russian government, to the police, to get our transit papers. They didn't like you to leave their perfect country, you could get Siberia, could get prison, disappear, dead, shot, maybe worse. Came a day when I had to go in over there, *this is the NKVD,*[16] this is the *worst* ones. The only time when they worked was twelve o'clock at night–they take out somebody for troubles, to go to a court, anything, was done at night. In the daytime they don't want people to see. They ask questions, "How come?" I said, "Mine family lives in the States, but I have no one here, I got stuck." They didn't check up! did nothing! It takes about ten days and they'll give us a transit visa to go *through* Russia, but not *to live* in Russia, the "Golden Country," they called it.

After eight days I got a note to go there–Christmas night–you know they don't believe in nothing!–and get the papers. They give us our transit visas, and they said, "You have to leave Vilna, the 4th of January, 1941. Can't stay longer than four days in Lithuania any more, have to go, that's it, take your belongings and go!" You stay later, *they take you* to Siberia! That's how we got from them the transit visas to go over Russia to Japan. Mine friend Ruchleimer was older than me, he got cold feet, and I said, "If you break down now, it's going to be bad, are you going or not? go! I'm telling you, this is the time!" He didn't back out.

(When I came in to the NKVD to get mine papers, a man was sitting there with a moustache with a pair of glasses. I didn't know who he is or what he is, I didn't say one word to him. When I came to Japan I have seen that man again, he landed up in the same building as me, and then I said to mineself, "I'm not afraid of you, buddy, it's a free country, I have to know." We grabbed him and I said, "Listen, you tell us who you are, we don't trust you, you don't trust us, but we know something is going on." He took off that moustache and we find out he is smuggling with some other people diamonds from Poland to the Russian border. The Russians have captured somebody and that somebody squealed that this man is the one who handles all the diamonds and gold. He went on a trial: before the trial, they take you in a basement filled with water, two soldiers watching you, maybe you confess. You stay in the middle of the soldiers, they won't let you lean on the wall, you can't sit down, you can't go to sleep. They take you out early in the morning for a trial. This boy–six feet tall, husky boy–served in the Polish cavalry and when they took him out one Russian soldier is walking in the front with the bayonet–when they walk they held the rifle in a special way–but the soldier's half asleep–he's been up all night, too, you know–the other one was behind him, and he have seen that he too is a little bit sleepy. This man grabbed the soldier's rifle, shot this one, shot the other one and he took off. That's why there was so much money delegated to find out who did it–all kinds of posters handed out in places the Russian occupied, offered fifty thousand rubles to whoever reports for his head. Never find him. He went away to the States and I've never seen him again. Killed both Russian soldiers!)

Isaac Ruchleimer, he started to shiver. I said, "Don't shiver, we going, we decided we go, forget about it." We wanted to go by Intourist but they wanted dollars and you had to buy dollars in the black market and pay top price, and what did the Russians do? Before you walked into Intourist a detective from NKVD said, "What have you got in your pocket?" He showed you the badge, and took your dollars and you, too, so we got afraid to buy them or they'll arrest you and they'll say nobody can go no place. We decided we'll go for rubles, we had a lot of them. I sold what I could of the fur what I had stored away for rubles.

I wanted to take that family where I stayed. I told them, "If you want you can go out, come with me, I'll take you, it'll maybe save your life. We still have the stamp to make some visas." They didn't want to go with me, they have been afraid. This is the last I have seen of these people. I wrote them letters from Japan, never got a reply. I left everything what I didn't sell–all kinds of stuff, sheepskins, furs–with that family. I said, "Whatever is here you can have, sell, keep, save yourself, your life."

You know why they have been afraid? There was a lady–she had lived downstairs long before. She and her husband have been travelling in Russia and this woman, she made a joke about Stalin to a girlfriend, and the girlfriend turned her in, and she got ten years Siberia. Ten years! She worked there underground: in the morning they used to pick them up, then blindfolds, but they knew the air was different under the ground from on top–they used to take them early to work and then back in the evening, after ten-twelve hours. They made munitions, tanks. She had a baby boy born before she went to prison, she was with the baby for six months, and after they took away the baby and when she came out they give her back the boy what is hers–the boy didn't know the mother or nothing–and they said, "This is your boy." For good behaving they give her only nine years.

She said to me, "Chaimke, I heard that you're leaving Vilna, you're going across Russia, you're going away to America. Tell me the truth." I said, "Yes, I'm going away." I didn't tell her I had false papers. "I'm afraid something happens to you. Be careful," she said, "they will take you off from the train, you will get lost, I've never seen mine husband anymore." I said, "I'm going to go! I have to go! Can't stay here! that's all! Good-bye." But I couldn't forget when I have been travelling over Russia what she told me, what has happened to her from the Russians.

She said, "You taking any clothes?" I said, "I am taking all sorts of stuff, and everything what I got is brand-new." I had gloves, socks, suits, warm underwear, boots. In Vilna I bought sweaters–the Lithuanians made beautiful white pullovers, pure wool, I must have had about four or five–I sold that in Vladivostok. We had some clothes for ourselves, and a few watches–I figured if you get stuck somewhere, to Russians it was a big something. We bought a lot of fruit, salamis, hard bread what doesn't go bad, cheese. We went with whatever we could. We carried big suitcases!

We went down on the station on the 4th of January, 1941, and we bought tickets to Minsk. We left on the 4th of January, four o'clock in the evening. Took about four hours. In Minsk we had to transfer for the Moscow train.

Chapter VI

We arrive in Moscow

"If you want to buy yourself something here there's nothing to buy."

We got to Moscow, we took a bus to the Nova Moskovska Hotel–Tourist Hotel–near the Kremlin. We had luggage, but we didn't have a hotel booked up, nothing, we're going to get a room. We came to the Tourist Hotel and they asked me, "How come you don't have a room?" and I said, "We didn't know, we don't have dollars, we don't have where to buy them, Russian money is the best money in the world." That's what we told them–they liked to hear that! (On the desk there's a red light you can't recognize the people who you're talking to and they can't recognize you either, the man at the desk says red light is a special make.)

In that hotel lobby we see a lot of Jewish boys, rabbis and students–I know some of them, I met them in Vilna. The Japanese consul give some of them visas, and they went just like that to Moscow, but others don't have. (I don't know how they got to Moscow.) In Moscow they decide to go from Moscow to Turkey and from Turkey go into Palestine, but they need the visas to Turkey. They find out the Turkish government gives out visas but they didn't like to give out. So the boys decide to make for themselves visas. They had a boy make the stamp, but they need Turkish paper, special paper, had a watermark, half a moon and a star. (Somebody had a visa, got through, notified some of the boys that at the Turkish border when they check you, they only look at the paper to see the watermark. He told them, "Don't be afraid, when you get to the Turkish border, don't say nothing, they don't ask nothing, they just take your visa and look up at it with the light and if it's their paper with the moon and star you go through and that's all.")

These boys walked into the Turkish Embassy in Moscow, they asked to see the Consul and they find out that in this-and-this desk drawer is laying stacks of the special Turkish paper. Then some boys went down again to the Embassy, talk to the Consul to take his mind away and others got out a bundle of the papers, and went out, back to the hotel. Two boys came over to me–I knew them very well–they said, "Chaim, you have maybe some ink? Waterman's ink? The Russians' ink, it looks like no good, the Turks would recognize that." Russian ink is different from anybody else's, and the boys couldn't sign the papers with that. Waterman's ink was the best. I said, "I have a small bottle of that." I said, "You got a pen?" A pen they had. I filled up mine Parker pen and give them the bottle of Waterman's ink, and said, "You can have it." (I wouldn't give away that pen–it was a present from mine father. Before the war he had given it to me. Later on the boat to Japan I was so hungry I give it away for a bowl of soup!) And after Ruchleimer and I left Moscow, the boys made out the visas right there in the hotel!

The boys said to me, "Chaimke, if you want, you can change your mind, we have enough papers," but I can't change mine mind to go a different way, I had already mine papers to go to Japan. (All them boys went to Turkey. The Turkish government didn't look at the signatures or nothing, they looked in the light at the paper if there is a star in the moon in the watermark and that's how every one of them came into Israel. In fact, these boys, they have been the first to tell mine brother Noah in Palestine that they have seen me in Moscow going to Japan.)

Ruchleimer and I got a room already, put away our luggage. Mine friend Ruchleimer–who was a great musician playing violin–he said, "We'll wash a little bit and, Chaimke, we'll go see an opera–I'd like to see an opera in Moscow." I said, "You go to hell with opera." I said, "Don't bother with opera–who cares about opera?–it's not in mine mind!"

But Ruchleimer asked the head man who sits at the desk if we can get two tickets to the opera. The man whispers to us, "Listen, do you speak Yiddish?" We say, "Yes." He says, "Don't talk." And he wrote things down: "Havera (means comrade in Yiddish, but like friend, not communist) take belongings and go, if not they will find you. Right away, step on the gas, make feet. Don't bother with opera, you'll never come out from over there." Just like that! What should we do? "How do we go?" He didn't talk but he wrote down in Jewish–he knows we don't read the Russian language–Ruchleimer speaks but didn't read–"You take a taxi from here to the Yaroslavl Station over there on Komsomol Square, buy tickets direct to Vladivostok, to no other places, if not they'll take you off and you'll never find. If they don't want to give you tickets to Vladivostok direct, give under the table." We had been loaded with Russian money and he says, "You'll take a cab from here and if you want to buy yourself something here there's nothing to buy but just go and don't say nothing."

He took that paper he'd written on and burned it up under a candle (the lights in that hotel have been such a colour you couldn't recognize anybody so he had a candle), scrunched it up, and walked into the toilet and flushed it down, finished. So we took our luggage down from our room, give a tip to the doorman for a cab. The cab driver sees we had leather gloves, good ones, and says, "I don't want any money from you if you can give me a pair of them." (I had about four or five pair of gloves, I had prepared mineself, if I have to sell or trade or something.) Mine friend Ruchleimer spoke the Russian language. I said, "I'll give you a watch." He said he don't want a watch, he wants a pair of gloves, so we give him. (We've seen the people have been very poorly dressed in Russia, in Moscow.)

We came down to the station and the ticket lady says she can't give us direct a ticket to Vladivostok, we have to get off at every station and get a new ticket. I says, "We don't know where to go or how or what!" We took out a thousand rubles and give to her quietly–people didn't have to know what's going on–"Here's for you, young lady." And we paid her for two tickets direct to Vladivostok and we got on the train. We were in Moscow maybe one hour.

We left at night.

Chapter VII

We go across on the Trans-Siberian

"It's hard to believe I fooled Stalin–if he knew he would commit suicide!"

In the train there was laying boards and on the boards was laying mattresses from straw, and I was afraid I'd get lice. (I didn't–I watched myself.) They give us a straw pillow. That's where we sat and slept–that was second class! There were bunks, Ruchleimer was on the top and I was on the bottom. We went eleven days and eleven nights to Vladivostok, and we took enough food for all that time.

We put away our suitcases. We opened up something to eat but we didn't show people what we have, close it up fast, nobody should see, they would murder you for that food what we carried out from Lithuania–salamis and sardines and cheeses, fruit and black bread. People had to bring their own tea and food. And you should see the clothes! Washing facilities? Just a toilet and a sink to wash the hands but the water would freeze when you're going through Siberia, when it's very cold. I used to take a shave every three days, change socks or something, take off a shirt, wash your face. We kept our eyes open that nobody steals our belongings. (I didn't take off mine shoes the whole trip, I was afraid someone would steal them right away!) When the train stopped at a station, we have been afraid to go on the platform, we have been afraid every time, we didn't know whether they would let you back on. It was cold, 40 below zero. We didn't see much–the only places we got off the train were at Irkutsk and Birobijan. We have been always on guard. Any time, any time, they could come on the train and take you out, nothing to stop them, they could take who they wanted, get ten years Urals, labour camp, maybe get shot.[17] This was the enemy!

The train stopped a lot to get water, coal. There was snow, snow, and snow. When we stopped at the stations you couldn't buy nothing, the only thing you could get was boiled water, that was free. Boiled hot water, bring your own tea! They had leaves from trees, lipova herbata–a herb tea–a little leaf and in the middle is like three little things hanging out. And that was life under Stalin! And after they got in the war. If it wouldn't be for the United States, England, Canada, giving all that help, they would have lost the war.

We travelled over Siberia. When we went deeper in Siberia, we saw people–refugees from Poland, from other countries, they ran away from the Germans, taken by the Russians, they took them all out to Siberia. They lived under the ground, in holes, crawl in, no houses, all mud huts or holes.[18] They made bunkers in the field. They cut lumber–the more lumber you cut, the more bread you got.

If the Russians would have known I am a Polish Jew! I was going with Lithuanian papers, you know, I had a Lithuanian passport. (It was real. I lied to get it–Russians took all Polish Jews and other Poles, make them Soviet citizens.)[19] The conductors on the train feel that we are Germans–they think the Yiddish we talk is German–the Russians have been friends with the Germans then. It's hard to believe I fooled Stalin–if he knew he would commit suicide! Nobody knew that I rode with those papers. Now I wouldn't have the guts, but that time I had the guts, I was young. I said to mineself, "I am not going to serve in the Russian Army, serve Stalin, you know, and that's it!" and that's why I did it all.

We got off at the Irkutsk station, to catch a little bit breeze of air. It was past Siberia already. And the people have been begging if we had maybe some paper to write, pencils–they didn't have–that we can give them. You know what they had for exchange? Some frozen watermelon! I can't believe that! I'm not telling a lie, you know. And some of them had milk, goats' milk, or some kind–they didn't have in bottles, you had to have a container, they would pour it in for you. (When I see how they throw out containers and this and that here in Canada, it is impossible to believe what I have seen over there!)

The train started going up into the hills and they bring a locomotive in the back, and one goes in the front, till the mountains are gone. We came down to the Baikal Lake, the richest place in Russia, all kinds of oil and gas there. The conductor told us that during the Revolution, they blew up a few trains and they fell in the water and in summertime when you're looking into that water you can see the trains, you can throw a stone and see how the water's clear and it goes on to the bottom.

We came into Birobijan, which used to be a republic for Jews.[20] There was a sign in Russian: "This is the Jewish Republic of Birobijan." In Poland I read in a book about Jewish people here–the Communists want to make Jews into farmers, no more owning stores, they got rid of that–no more middlemen they called it–so they put them here. I talked to some people in Poland, and someone said, "After the Revolution the Russians put the Jews down there, but there was no place to make a living, so the people ran away and there was only a few hundred families left." I hear more Jews would leave than would come! Heh! Later Kruschev says that Jews won't work on farms so that is why they left–he never heard of a kibbutz!? And Stalin killed a lot of them, the leaders, he made a purge, not just Jews, everybody. But just Jewish leaders in Birobijan.

We came into a station, a city, they called it Bira, maybe about forty kilometres before Birobijan the city. A man came up on the train in Bira, his wife holds him by the hand, and he was blind. He was playing the violin. He played all kinds of songs. He begs from one station to the other someone should give him something, he plays for a piece of bread. He came into our wagon and we asked him, "What nationality are you?" He says he's Jewish. They had three sons: one son got killed in 1940 in Finland–the Russian-Finland War–one is in the Russian Army, and one is the head manager in a factory where they make shoes just for the army.[21]

He said, "We live in Birobijan. After the Revolution people couldn't pay taxes and there's nothing to do so they all spread out all over Russia." We asked him, "What did you do before the Revolution?" and he said he had one of the biggest businesses from import and export, used to bring in from other countries merchandise, fruit, to Vladivostok and used to ship it out all over Russia, exporting all kinds of things to other countries. "But then the Revolution came, and the Communists took away our business, no Jewish people in businesses, no businesses, so they make this place, a Jewish Republic, but everybody left, couldn't make a living." This man told us, "I turned blind and my family was here so I stayed." And he went on the train, for an hour he played, people give him something. In Birobijan we read there are thousands of Jews–don't believe it!– when I was there there's a hundred and eighty Jewish families.

I remember we asked him if he remembers the Kol Nidre, from the High Holidays, and he says he remembers but he didn't use it for years and years and years. Mine friend badly wanted to play the violin but he didn't want to bother the man, so I asked him if he could lend the violin for him to play. We give the man some money, and my friend took from him the violin–playing classical violin, that Ruchleimer–and he started to play Kol Nidre *(a prayer sung on the eve of Yom Kippur)* and the man cried. We give him two pair of gloves, and a salami–we had brought about ten salamis in a suitcase–we ate some of them– we had some special hard bread what doesn't get spoiled, we give him some of this, and some warm underwear. I had about six watches–for a watch I could have bought Stalin *with* his daughter–so I give him a watch, and he thanked us and he cried like a baby. And when we came to the city Birobijan he said good-bye and got off.

We had to wait in Birobijan Station, and so we asked the Station Master, "Can we go downtown?" He said, "The train is not going to wait for you." We ask, "When is the train leaving?" He said, "In our country we don't know when the train is coming, when the train is leaving!" And I said, "Can you get a newspaper here?" and he said, "You can't get nothing here!" On his desk was laying around a few pieces sugar, brown sugar–not finished–so I took a piece of that sugar, and I said, "How much is that?" and he said "Two rubles." So I took that brown sugar, no paper, no nothing and wrapped it in a piece of newspaper what I had in mine briefcase and that was the only thing I bought over there, what I had as a souvenir from the whole trip!

We waited about an hour. The women have been going around checking the wheel, it's oiled, about ten or fifteen women, no men, wasn't a man's job. They had big oil containers, filled up the axels with oil and then we left the station.

We had the right as tourists to go in the restaurant on the train–we went in every second day, we didn't want to spend so much money, we carried our own food, but we liked a change–nothing to do on the train. The Russian people, they couldn't go in the restaurant, only for tourists. They carried all their food, a little bit dark bread, they made a little bit tea, they fasted.

There was a boy on the train–a cadet from the Russian Army (you know, a young boy who becomes an officer), he had four weeks vacation but he's on the road more than two weeks and his father died. The mother worked in a hospital and the brother worked in a school. He spent two weeks travelling. He was a Jewish boy, we told him we are Jewish and we wanted to treat him with a dinner. (He was waiting for a station maybe he'll be able to buy something.) He didn't speak Yiddish–Ruchleimer talked to him in Russian. He came in with us to the restaurant and they told him to go out from the wagon. There have been many tourists on the train, going from Lithuania to Vladivostok, to try to get away–they could use the restaurant, he couldn't. What we did, there was a waiter and he was a Jewish boy–I recognized him as Jewish–he told us his name, he said he has an uncle in Israel, he give us the address in Haifa–I said, "Listen, sell me a meal for that boy, an extra one," and we give him twenty rubles and besides this we paid for the meal. They made for us an omelet from eggs, some dark bread, tea, and a piece of cake, poppy seed cake–that was the meal, they didn't have any meat. We brought him back that meal and he closed himself in and he cried. He said, "I'm a Russian soldier and I can't get anything to eat." And I felt very bad. And we travelled like that.

In Siberia, I was going to the washroom and a man grabbed me–I figured he was going to make a holdup or kill me or something, but he said, "Tovarich, you are going to America, tell the people we are waiting for a new revolution in our country." He has been in jail for being against the government. He was away for twelve years and now he's out, he's going back to his hometown.

We never made any conversation with people, we were afraid to start up, you didn't know who, when, and what and you had to keep your mouth shut, no paper, no book, and that's it, we sat and prayed.

Chapter VII

We wait in Vladivostok

"The Russian officer says, This you can take, this you can't take.'"

We came to Vladivostok around January 15, 1941, I think, and stayed in a tourist hotel there, and we waited for a boat. A Japanese boat is supposed to come but the Pacific is so rough in winter there that you sometimes wait months–we waited almost six weeks. What did we do to pass the time? played cards, read an old magazine, read a book, went to a movie–most of it was American films, but I don't remember the names.

I have seen we are starting to run out of money. We had to pay for a meal, the Russians wanted dollars, they didn't trust their own money! We had to buy dollars for rubles, we bought from Americans–at that time there was a lot of Americans over there, sailors, some of them had American money so they helped us out. We had one meal a day–we couldn't afford any more–and we paid top money for it! We helped out some Jewish students, too, they were students for rabbis, didn't have anything, any money, and they eat maybe every second day. Our money is going out fast. We decide to see about selling something–after all, that's why we brought all that stuff!

We went downtown–in downtown Vladivostok was one street, called Lenin Street, had laying for sidewalks boards, in the mud, and there was very few stores, it's not developed, there was hardly nothing. We went in one store, had wood cupboards, there was Russian people in there, women, men, and there was barrels with herring. You bought yourself a herring–bread you had under the arm, bought somewhere in a bakershop–and the soldiers used to hit the herring over the boots to take off the salt and eat that, and drink homemade, not finished-up, vodka. You maybe could drink that vodka with that herring–I couldn't!

The day came that in a week's time there's going to be a boat for Japan, and we waited, and we waited, and the money was going, going. I had those beautiful clothes, pure stuff, officers' goods: I had two pairs special officers' pants, warm boots–officers' boots–and I had all kinds of pullovers, all wool–turtlenecks I had brought from Lithuania–they made beautiful stuff there. I took a bunch and went down to a store–a special store what the government runs, the government buys and sells–no private stores–and they offered me hardly nothing: the woman says she's going to give me 700 rubles for everything! Somebody pinched me in mine back and I almost yelled. The lady who pinched me whispers, "Don't give it to them. I'll give you more money." She have seen what I have showed the woman. I walked out with those two big parcels of clothes, and she give me about seven thousand rubles–they'd offered me seven hundred! I dropped the parcels and she took. Maybe she sells it later and makes something for herself, maybe she uses for her family. I didn't ask.

There was another lady, she give us a haircut and shave, I sold her some of our razors–she says, "I'll give you anything if you could sell me that razor." They couldn't get that. There wasn't much to buy in Russia, nothing good, so people bought from others, like these ladies. I had a lot of stuff, people told me in Vilna, "Chaim, have everything prepared! Take as much as you can!"

The boat came. We packed up our bags. We were on our way to Japan! But before we went on the boat, the Russians took me in a room (like we have here, Customs), everybody was separated, and the Russians took off from me a lot of stuff. I had still all kinds of new shirts, underwear, socks, nice clothes–but the officer said, "This you can take, this you can't take." I said, "Take everything you want, but I have to have something to change." And I said, "Leave me mine pictures, you don't need them." They left me with a little bit, the rest they confiscated. I came to Japan with one suit, some underwear, a few handkerchiefs–the watches I sold in Vladivostok.

On the streets of Vladivostok you couldn't get nothing to buy. The only thing I bought was stamps, Russian stamps, old ones, and when I was in Customs the Russian officer said, "What is this?" I said, "I bought this for a souvenir from Russia." He said he didn't need it. When I came to Canada, I sold them, I got a few dollars for them–whenever you are in a country and you can't take out money, buy stamps.[22]

There was Ruchleimer and me, and there were about forty or fifty boys, maybe more. The Japanese boat was the Amakusa Moru. I went first, and we made a signal: if it's okay I'll hold mine hat in mine hand, off mine head–I had a hat like an airplane pilot's hat I bought in Vilna–that everybody should go straightaway, not to be afraid. It was okay for me, I held mine hat, they saw it, they came on board. The Japanese officer was standing here and the captain was standing there, and he looked a little at the papers, said, "Go ahead," and all the boys came aboard ship. (We find out later in Japan that the whole bunch of Jewish boys had all the same visas made! Identical! But the Japanese knew we are running away from Communism and that's the reason they didn't catch anybody–they wouldn't look close.) And we all made it!

Before I went on the boat, the Russian Immigration man said, "If you want you can change your mind, you can stay in Sovietsky Sayuse–in our big country–it's got everything, gold and diamonds and milk and honey like life in the Holy Land!" I said, "I thank you very much," and went aboard. (But I am still afraid that the Russians will come and take me off.)

Finally, about 12:30 in the afternoon–I think maybe end of February–the Japanese captain orders to bring out the tugboat from port. The Russian pilots take out the boat to the sea, leave the boat and take the tugboat back and we left. When the tugboat got back to Vladivostok and left us, it was the happiest day for me. And I thanked the Lord.

From Russia to Japan we lay on the floor on straw. (After I hear that the boat what I came on from Russia to Japan later split in half from the waves–it was not in good shape!) The Pacific was rough, but I didn't have nothing to throw up. I was hungry! But I had no money and didn't have any merchandise left. Finally I thought, "I have mine Parker pen," and I said to mine friend, "I'm going to buy a bowl of soup for us here." And the Japanese give us bowls of soup for the golden Parker pen I had, what mine father give me. I give them that Parker pen and we got two bowls of rice, with octopus, whatever it was inside I eat–I didn't know myself–I was so hungry. I asked him after for a refill and he give it to us.

After about forty hours we arrived in Tsuruga, the first port in Japan, and I said, "Is this a dream or something?" And then they announced we cannot land, we have to go back to Russia, we haven't got visas to go out from Japan! and they didn't want to keep us. The Japanese Immigration said, "Sorry, we can't let you in, you have just transit visas and you haven't got where to go after that. We are at war with China and we can't leave you off there." The Japanese give us an order, "You have to leave Japan." After forty-eight hours we had to go back to Russia!

We didn't get off the boat, we waited, they feed us whatever they have–not enough, wasn't a passenger boat, was a cargo boat. I looked at the land, and went out just to the shore, took a little bit ground and put it in a hanky. I kissed the hanky and I went back on board and the Japanese looked at me, if I'm meshugah *(crazy in Yiddish).* The boat has to go back to Vladivostok. The people brought on board fruit for us. Japanese I couldn't talk, English I couldn't speak, the Japanese laughed when I put the dirt in the handkerchief and they give us some fruit!

And when we came back to Vladivostok, they actually sent down a boat special with a doctor, two doctors, women doctors, and they asked, "Who's sick?" If you're sick they'll take you off and they'll give medicine or something. But nobody was sick, nobody went out on the deck and they put on projectors with lights and they put all kinds machine guns around that boat, nobody will escape. And we waited and next day came a big lot of Jewish people from Germany, and they have visas to go to Shanghai and we didn't. But HIAS *(Hebrew Immigrant Aid Society)* takes care of Jews going to other countries–let the world know that we were on the boat, and they made special arrangements, they got together with the Government of Ecuador, made us visas to go to Ecuador, to leave us in Ecuador. We left again for Japan on the boat to go now to Ecuador–and we can stay for a while in Japan, in Kobe. We were in the middle of the ocean, we were going back to Japan and our destination is Ecuador! (But the visas were a fake! HIAS made them so we could go to Japan.)

We come again to Tsuruga, we landed, we got off. I looked around, women have been walking around carrying baskets of coal for the boat, half naked up top, and I figured, "I don't fit into this nation!" What was I doing here? But I was here. Ruchleimer and I and the other boys had survived. We got away from the Russians!

Chapter IX

We Wait In Japan

"I carried out very good memories of the Japanese people."

We got off the boat and we went from Suruga by train to Kobe. Kobe was a nice city, very clean. Through the Jewish community–there *was* a Jewish community in Japan, in Kobe–they give us a place where to live. The Japanese give us bread, made from rice–you know I could eat up two loaves of that bread! We arrive in March, 1941, and I left in June.[23]

The worst thing is I didn't have any money. (I have five dollars American stuffed away in a little pocket that no one could find it–I travelled with this from Lithuania, for an emergency. I did use it in Japan about three days after I came there, for food, for me and Ruchleimer.) HIAS give us–give everybody–a little money to have a few pennies in the pocket, but it wasn't enough to survive. They give us a house–here was about ten or twelve families in that house. (I remember the address like now: Shirouchi 2, Kobe.) The HIAS put on a Jewish man to look after the house and mine friend Ruchleimer and I, we asked him for a job. "Can we work in this house for refugees where we are staying?" and he said, "Boys, you can't make much money." We said, "We don't need much." He said, "What would you like to do?" We said, "Any kind of work you give us, we'll do it!" so we divided–I worked in the kitchen and mine friend cleaned the hallways, the washrooms. We made four yen a day–that's about fifty cents each. The fire had to be made up five o'clock in the morning, so I had to get up early. Then I washed the kitchen and made the fifty cents. I looked after the kitchen, the people shouldn't fight–over hot water or something.

I delivered laundry for Mr. Kowalski, a very well-to-do man, a refugee, the biggest dealer from cattle and horses in the Old Country. He came out from Japan–I don't know where he went–Brazil? New Zealand? after I left. At night it costs me five cents to go into a special place to take a bath, every night, not a steam bath, you go in and wash yourself first and after they had mineral water in a small basin, and finished. I went to give the lady the five cents. She knows we are refugees, we haven't got, so she didn't take the five cents–she showed me by the hand she wouldn't take it. In the barbershop too, I went–beautiful barbershops, had ladies to cut–you know the men had been away in the army, you didn't see–whatever it costs she always give me back. So I carried out very good memories of the Japanese people, very generous.

From Japan I sent tea to Poland, to mine family–with tea you could buy anything in Poland then–and they got every package of tea. I didn't put mine name on–the Japanese company put their name on, they didn't want to have any problems. Whatever money I made I went down to a big store and asked them if they could send packages of tea, a pound, and it went. (The Germans didn't try to destroy that on account it came from Japan, they have been allies. And you could write letters from there–I wrote my cousin Chaim Goldberg in Israel, from Japan the letter took, I don't know how, three four months. A lot of letters went through Turkey.) Did it bother me that the Japanese and Germans were Allies? It bothered me and I couldn't believe mine eyes how nice they treated us! But I was young and there was so much to see, to do, there in Japan.

When I joined the Polish Army in Japan the Polish Government give me fifty dollars and I give ten dollars to the export house to send every two weeks a parcel of tea to mine father's address–and every package of tea arrived. I know because I have a friend now in Israel, name Wiener, lived then still in Pulawy, and after the war I met him and he says, "Hy, the mailman was going to your father's house and we have seen four or five packages and they had to sign that they have delivered it." They knew it comes from me, from Japan, but they couldn't write–no address, just the tea company. I never heard from anyone in mine family again, never.

A lot of times I've seen the young Japanese boys walking by the house we lived in going to a club, they played there ping pong. When I was a young boy I enjoyed it so I went in and watched and watched and one says, "*'Cominay'*–means 'Mister'–you want to, go ahead," so he give me his racket and I played a few times with this one and that one, you know, so I've got good memories. They play soccer, too, and baseball is a big thing to them, like in America.

In Kobe we stayed a few months, but the Japanese said, "We can't keep you here, you have to leave to go to Shanghai on account we can't feed you here, we haven't got."[24] I decided I'm not going to go to Shanghai because there are letters from boys who've gone to there and they said, "If you won't better commit suicide don't come to Shanghai, dead people on the streets at night, in the morning comes a truck–a dump truck–and they throw them in, and that's all. And that river what goes through Shanghai, you find dead people swimming around, they bring them out, put them on the dump trucks." I have seen Ruchleimer got an order to leave Japan to go to Shanghai and I says to myself, "That's not for me." I says to him, "If you want, Ruchleimer, come with me, we have been going together for so long, we never got lost, I am younger, you older, you know what to do better." But he couldn't do it.

The Polish Government wanted to get out as many young Polish men as they can to the army, so they told quietly, "If you are 19-20 years of age, we'll give you a Polish passport, you'll go to Canada, you'll keep your mouth shut, nobody has to know." The Polish Government got in touch with us, said, "Listen, you have to keep your eyes open, your ears open, your mouth shut, not to mention to the Japanese you are going to the army, you are going instead to families." I hear that they form a Polish Army in Canada and I decided I am going to go, I wanted to be in the army and see the German cowards dead in mine lifetime and that's all I wanted. But the Japanese don't have to know, nobody. The Polish

Government give me a ticket to go for an examination, if I'm healthy—a Polish doctor, *he* knew I was going in the army. They have seen that I am fit, so the Polish Government give me fifty dollars and a passport.[25]

But Ruchleimer was too short and too old—he was maybe fifteen years older than me—for the Polish Army. So mine friend went to Shanghai where he was dealing for a piece of bread. He wrote to me he was happy that I had left and survived. (After the war he came from Shanghai to New York—they give you a time to leave Shanghai, there was a boat going to the United States and a lot of the refugees got on that boat—that was in 1946. He came to see me in Detroit. In New York he opened up a place from pearls and he used to go to Japan to bring back pearls. This girl worked for him and he married her—I went to New York for his wedding—and they had four kids. His sister lives in Israel, she came from Russia after the war.)

I carried out the best memories about the Japanese people, they are a very fine, intelligent nation. They give us a place where to live, they give us bread. They treated us very nice wherever we went—the Japanese had a very big respect for us. They know we are refugees. They had such beautiful cities, big stores, the people very polite, you come in a streetcar they give you a chance. On a streetcar I went to give a lady mine place—she was carrying the baby in the back, you know—and a man says to me, "No, she can stand, you can sit," but I don't like that, after all I'm a European man, so I got up.

A Japanese passenger boat, the *Hikawa-Maru*, was going to Canada. I said good-bye to mine friend Ruchleimer and I left. The Polish Government paid for the fare. The Japanese didn't know that we were getting organized to go to fight the Germans, their allies. This boat was going to the United States, stopped first in Seattle, Washington.

I can't forget that when we left Japan, the people brought flowers, threw flowers, an orchestra played. It was a regular passenger ship. Quite a few boys went with me. Most of the Jews in Japan left, for Canada, the States, Australia, New Zealand, South America, India. I was in the first group to leave.

Mine God, I was so sick on the Pacific! you have never seen—not as sick as later on the Atlantic. Going from Russia to Japan, sea-sickness didn't bother me. In the middle of the ocean, the *Hikawa-Maru* stopped, the sailors came down in small boats hanging on the sides. They spent hours in maneuvers, with semaphores, with signals, and we didn't go till they came back and they lift the boats up and I said to mineself, "Mine god, where did they get so many boats? I have never seen in mine life so many boats!" I woke up and said to mineself, "Something's going to happen." When I went to school they told us the Japanese lived from a little bit rice and a little bit fishing, and they live all in little boats, and that's it! On that ocean, I said to mineself, "Am I crazy?"

In Poland we knew only a little bit about the rest of the world—in those days you didn't know so much as now—we knew that the Japanese are fighting in Mongolia, fighting the Chinese. We knew that, but we didn't know that they are equipped with such airplanes—you should have seen the sky, it was black. On the ship—hard to believe—the airplanes, you didn't see them on the top, they had them on the bottom, they came up over the deck, you couldn't spot them, everything was down under, and when they took out four or five, they lift them up, the deck opened up, they got them out—never saw that before. They have been equipped! they have been equipped!

Chapter X

Mine brother Noah

"Mine brother Noah survived because he went to Palestine."

Mine oldest brother Noah was a tailor, and in Poland in the middle of the thirties he didn't have enough work to make a living.[26] There came a time he didn't have what to do and some of his friends were going to Palestine–the British wouldn't let people in, so they went not legal.[27] Mine brother served in the Polish Army two years and when he came back from the army there was no work and he decided he's going away. He told the family, and the family said, "If you can better yourself, go ahead." But he didn't go yet. One day in summer time, the captain where he served in the army (who was a very fine friend of his) sent some soldiers to our home town in Pulawy, they are looking for mine brother, and in a small city people know right away. "The captain wants to see you, he is staying six kilometres away from here." Noah took a bicycle, went down, and the captain said, "Listen, Noah, we are going away on manoeuvres and we have a lot of uniforms you have to fix up for the soldiers. You can get yourself another tailor or two and you'll have enough work for a whole summer."

Noah worked the whole summer–used to bring home black bread from the army, whatever he wanted–and he got paid very good. (That captain was captured by Stalin, he was a prisoner of war in Russia, and after Sikorski[28] made a pact with Stalin to take out the Polish soldiers. He came out from Russia through Iran and to Palestine, and he remembered mine brother.)

Time was going on, winter was coming in–there was no work for tailors in Poland–and mine brother finally decided he's going to Palestine now. This was around 1935 or so. He went from Warsaw to France by train, as a tourist. In France we had an uncle, a fine man, a great swimmer, Jack Goldberg–they called him Jack but his real name was Jaker–mine father's brother. Mine uncle said, "Listen, Noah, I've nobody here, mine son is in Le Havre, mine daughter is not here, stay with us," but Noah said, "I have already mine forged papers." So mine uncle give him some money, "Look, you'll need it on the road, you haven't got."

From France they had special people took him out. (There was fellows, they made a group, they went as film people, as tourists, as book writers–that's how they travelled, how they fooled the Syrians, the British.) Special boat sailed from France, went to Beirut, and from Beirut they smuggled them into Syria. Noah didn't have papers to go into Palestine, the British wouldn't give out.

They've been in a hotel in Syria. One day they got a message: they went on a "tour"–left everything, all their equipment, suitcases, whatever they had. They never went back to the hotel. If you go out from a hotel you have to leave your passport, so they had no papers, not even the fake ones. A fellow took them on that "tour" and everybody went in different directions–the leaders knew what they were doing–they sent out messages to friends, and Noah was dropped off in the mountains where is the grave of Trumpeldor[29] the big fighter–he lost a hand fighting for the Russians against Japan–with the other hand he fought the Arabs, and when he died over there they made a memorial–called it in Hebrew Tel Hai. Two friends found out Noah was there from a young girl–her brother came to pick her up, and he called Noah's friends.

New Year's night, he was laying hiding on that grave of Trumpeldor and two boys came along with a taxi, with flashlights, and they said, "Are you Goldberg?" and he said, "Yes, and there's another boy hiding here." They got them in the cab, paid off the Syrian guard–on the borders there if you put in an English pound, that's enough, but there are lots of them to pay–and they took them to Tel Aviv. He came with just what he wore, just what he had, left everything, without even a piece of paper. About sixty people went on tour with Noah, and they all got into Palestine, one here, two there, all separate. But the British didn't like, and they made trouble.

He had a hard time in Palestine, he didn't have what to do, he didn't have what to eat, and it was very bad. People wear short pants, people didn't care to be dressed, no work for a tailor! I was making good money in Warsaw, and I find out that mine brother Noah is struggling in Palestine. But you couldn't send out money from Poland. Mine boss Mr. Preminger used to travel to go buy sheepskins, so I said, "Mr. Preminger, I can't send any money from Poland, but you're going to Yugoslavia, Rumania, you're going to Bulgaria, if you can send out to mine brother Noah in Palestine, four pounds"–a pound was at the time twenty-five zlotys–for one English pound you could buy a lot of stuff in Palestine, live over there very good. So I used to send with Mr. Preminger. One day I got a letter, "Dear Brother, when I got the four pounds, it was just like four thousand dollars in mine pocket. The first thing, I bought mineself two shirts, four pair of socks, and I went to eat a meal. For four pounds I could live for a long time, everything is very cheap."

He went to work in a small factory, they made pants and jackets. He stayed with a friend who was a baker. At night Noah used to go to the bakershop to wash–he didn't have water where he stayed, water was a big thing there–he'd crawl in the window. One night he put on the soap and a man came out with a long beard and says, "I'm giving you over to the British, you got in illegal." The man was the landlord of the bakershop. He didn't like Noah using his water. Noah says, "Let me wash up that soap, mister, please." He wouldn't let him wash it off, mine brother struggled with him, and Noah got away with the soap on still. He went to some boys who have been in the Haganah,[30] and two men came right away and they told that man with a beard, "If you give one of our boys to the British, your head is going to hang in your synagogue with your beard. You'll hang in Tel Aviv in the main street." After that they watched that man that he never give away anybody.

A little later mine brother had a small tailor place where he worked with his partner–he had an upstairs and the stars he could see through the roof and if it rains they put pails–they couldn't afford to pay the rent, the landlord wouldn't fix.

There came a couple of boys talking Polish, looking around for a Goldberg on Allenby Street. They have been going around, looking, looking, and one says to the other, "You see that tailor shop upstairs? maybe that's the place." They went up there and handed Noah a letter that their captain from Poland wanted to see him, that he's outside Tel Aviv in a camp especially built for soldiers coming from Russia. Noah went there the same day. Turned out the same captain what Noah served in the army, this the captain who asked him to sew uniforms in Poland!

He wanted Noah to fix up the uniforms, the people looked like animals, they just had what to get out of Russia. After the war broke out, the Russians took away thousands of men in the Polish Army and made them prisoners. Sikorski signed a pact with the Russians and they let some out. (They killed a lot of them but we didn't find out till after–about the ones at Katyn, about other ones.)[31] They came to Palestine–because it was British–through Iran.

The captain says, "Listen, Noah, I got a lot of work for you, you can handle it? We have here a lot of boys." You know, the Russians steal everything, give them boys something just to cover the body but to look like a person they have to fix it. The captain says, "Listen, I want you to take as much as you can handle, hire yourself a few people to fix up. Go from one company to another, but first see that the officers have decent clothes." Noah had work for day and night, he hired about ten tailors he knew didn't have work, they made pants, straightened up this, that one jackets, another one blouses, other one shirts. Officers came around to fix their uniforms to look decent and this is when he made a living.

When Israel became a country, he made uniforms for the Israeli army, he made for Moshe Dayan–he used to get dressed from his place–Yitzak Rabin, Ben Gurion, he and his partner knew all the people. A lot of men went overseas from the Israeli Army, so they come to him, they have to be dressed decent, he got all kinds of diplomas for making their clothes. He had even a lot of rabbis used to come to make the big coats.

After the war, a man in mine regiment named Adam Pietras–not Jewish–was going back to Poland. I said, "Pietras, I'll tell you what, here's ten dollars American, and some Polish money, and things," and I give him some jackets, undershirts, other things–I bought special from some Canadian boys, they've been going home. "Here's an address where I lived, and if you will do me a favour I'll remember you." (He came from Brazil and he wanted to see his family in Poland. He went to join the army in Canada–they tell him the boat is going to land in Canada but they didn't, they turned around and landed in Liverpool! From over there he went to the Polish Army.) I asked him, "Can you tell me if anybody survived from mine family?" He wrote me, "Nobody survived, everybody's gone." He wrote me a letter that he went down to Pulawy and met a friend of mine that went with me to school, a Jewish boy, he was in the Polish Army under the Russian Government fighting the Germans. Pietras said, "Listen, mister, can you tell me where I can find this family," and mine friend cried, "Mine god! this is mine friend that went with me to school." Mine friend from school wrote me a letter, "Hy, nobody left from your family." Pietras wrote me one letter, "Hy, I wish you good luck, if you come to Poland, come look me up."

Around 1950 we went to a wedding in Detroit, and there was a man who told us how mine father and sisters died. He said, "I was going to the gas chamber with them together, and somebody started to shoot, the people before me went, and your father and sisters went, to the gas chamber. I have seen it. I got away." Mine three sisters and father and mine aunts and uncles and cousins–everybody went into the gas chamber. And that's what happened. Mine brother Noah survived because he went to Palestine. From mine family only mine brother Noah survived.

From some Polish boys who have been in the service I heard that mine other brother Scholem was in the hospital–I don't know why, I haven't got any reports–and an SS man came and somebody told mine brother that the SS man is going to do something to him, take him away maybe.[32] So mine brother grabbed the gun from the SS man, and shot him first, then shot himself, and died in the hospital.

In Israel Noah married Hannah, she was from Poland too. Her family was very well-to-do, the British have let them through–people with money, the British let them in to make work for others.[33] They had two daughters, Sarah and Judith, and they each have two children. And they are all in Israel.

Did I ever think of going to Palestine? No, I never wanted. Noah wanted to bring mine other brother Scholem to Palestine but the war broke out and he didn't finish the papers. When the war was over I asked Noah if he wanted me to come join him there. "No," he says, "you can help me better in a different country." After the war, life in Israel was very hard, I had to send him things, money, I could do it better from here.

Chapter XI

I join the Polish Army in Canada

"I was always hungry till I came to Canada!"

We arrived in Vancouver sometime in June 1941. I didn't know really what is what–what is Canada–when we came here. I just thought, "It's a big country!" I figured it's a wild country, there is more bush than land, you travel miles and miles and miles and you don't see a house! And it's true!

When we came down there in Vancouver we have been hungry! the Japanese on the boat they didn't give you much to eat–they didn't have, they watched themselves–so when we came to Vancouver they put on a big dinner for us: roast of beef, potatoes, bread, whatever you want. It disappeared in no time! Healthy husky boys, they could eat–that included me too, you know! The chef in that kitchen told our Jewish people from the Vancouver community, "I haven't got enough money to feed them people, they don't give me enough, Immigration doesn't give me enough to feed them!" He asked the community if they can help out with feeding. The Jewish community give money, and they feed us really good. I'll never forget that. The first day, everything disappeared in no time, the second day the same thing, on the third day we started leaving a little bit. They feed us to here and I wasn't hungry any more. (I was always hungry till I came to Canada!)

We stayed in Vancouver for about three days, they checked our papers. We stayed in a government hotel for immigration, and after we left on the train. We have been about forty or fifty boys, all Jewish boys, all going to the Polish Army, we didn't know where. We were on the train going from Winnipeg towards Windsor, Ontario, when we heard–the conductor came around and give us the news–that the Germans attacked Russia and that was the happiest day from mine life! June 22nd! I thought: the beginning of the end for both of them! (I thought, but wasn't true for Russia.

The headquarters of the Polish Army was in Windsor, in the lowest part of Ontario, across a river from Detroit–they shipped us to there, the whole group of boys, they formed a Polish Army there. (The Polish Government thought Polish boys from America, from Detroit and Chicago, would join up with the Polish Army in Windsor,[34] but they went into the American Army.) We have been the first.

The Jewish Community in Windsor made a dance, we were asked to go over there, and I says to somebody, "Look, we'll be dummies, we don't speak English and they don't understand Yiddish and they don't understand Polish." And he says, "Come on, Hy, we'll go over there and that's it." And that's how I met Ruth–

I married her after the war. But the girls–nice good-looking girls–didn't want to look at Polish boys, good-looking boys.

Ruth Goldberg: When we went in, they said, "You have to speak Polish or Jewish." I said to my girlfriend, "That's not for me, let's leave," but she said, "Oh, let's stay awhile, we're here." Ruth says she did speak some Yiddish–but Hy says, "One word! we couldn't talk, very little, she didn't understand."

We stayed maybe a month and a half in Windsor. On the street where used to be a typing company, make typewriters–they took this factory over and we had a barracks there, and then we went to Owen Sound and had all kinds of manoeuvres, exercises. We build barracks and beds and kitchens for other volunteers. Every day came new people. They teached us how to take apart machine guns, drilling, other training. All the boys were still together, with Polish officers, in the Polish Army, but we had Canadian uniforms. We had guard duty and the time went very fast by.

The best thing I enjoy, we used to eat in a restaurant–we didn't have a kitchen yet–and the man with the meals, he had a special room for us. He said, "All you boys eat like horses!" He said, "I'll tell you, I enjoy serving you! but I would better clothe you than feed you boys!" I used to enjoy that cornflakes with milk like you have never seen. I was eating every day cornflakes! Canadian food! I enjoyed every bit of it! I was never hungry in the army since I came to Canada. (Later I was hungry in Scotland in the service, they give you whatever they could, they didn't have for themselves there.)

In Owen Sound I was almost three months. Right after the High Holidays *(ten days from Rosh Hashanah to Yom Kippur)* came an order that the boys are going to England. They asked me if I'm satisfied, they said, "Do you want to go?" and I said, "I'm going and that's it." We took the train to Halifax and from Halifax a ship, but we had to come back, we had been already three days out and we had to come back on account of a blockade from submarines. I was excited! I came on the *Queen Mary* or some beautiful boat–the ship never had a name, all the names have been shut off–and I had the best place to sleep, a beautiful bed. There was a man by the name of Max Rosenstahl, a lawyer, and he had a bed to sleep on the floor. I said, "Look, Max, I'll tell you something, I'm young and you older than me"–Max must be over thirty–"you take mine bed and I'll sleep on the floor," and he was so happy that I give it to him and after that we have been best friends. We landed up in the same regiment in Scotland. Max couldn't take hold of a rifle when we had to change guard, he didn't have the way how to grab a rifle and present arms. I had a sergeant and he said, "Goldberg, you just came back from guard, you know, and I don't know what to do–Max Rosenstahl won't be able–do you want to go again?" and I said, "For Max I'll go if you don't mind." He just couldn't present arms–not that he was not willing, but it just didn't go and to me it was like playing a baseball bat over here. (I will never forget Max–anything I needed Max says, "Hy, you need something, I'll be glad to do for you." "Maxie, I don't need nothing." We lost track of each other after the war. When I was going on a trip to England later

I find out he's a lawyer in London, and I heard he was married and he had a son. I called him up, and I says, "Listen, are you Max Rosenstahl's son? I would like to talk to your father." And he says, "You're too late, my father passed away." But he survived the Germans and the war.)

I started in a tank regiment, but mine captain in Canada have seen me in the headquarters of the tank regiment and a few weeks after, I got a notice that Hy Goldberg is transferred to the 9th Infantry Battalion in Dalchise, six miles from Edinburgh. "Captain Judkowiak wanted you to be in his company." I says, "Captain, what happened here?" and he says, "Goldberg, I want you to be in mine company. I want you to look after the radio in mine jeep." Was I happy about this? I was pleased with everything–I volunteered and said to mineself, "I will make the best from everything. I have to see the Germans defeated."

Chapter XII

We train in Scotland

"We guarded the coasts of Scotland from the Germans."

We landed in Liverpool in September 1941 and went to Scotland. I have seen hills, mountains, sheep, and grass, nobody else, and there was some water. We stayed not far away from Glasgow, in a place by name Ellis, near Blayberry. The ladies made for us lessons, "Come to school if you want to learn English," so in the evening if I had time, I went for an hour. What English I learned is over there. We stayed in different places–we stayed in Dundee, Newport, Galahshields, Lamarck, Cooper–we guarded the coasts of Scotland from the Germans and we went in for exercises every day, every day. Mine general was Marian Kukiel. Mine division was in Scotland till July 1944, when we went to Normandy, end of July, after D-Day.

When I was in Scotland, stationed in Ellis, I went downtown with a few boys to have a beer and the English said to us, "Did you hear that the Japanese attacked the Americans at Pearl Harbor?" I couldn't believe, couldn't figure out, why this such nice nation is going against the United States! When we came from Japan, in Vancouver the press should have interviewed us, asked us what we knew. A lot of us could have told them the Japanese Navy is so big! That I have seen so many boats, nobody would believe! Some of the boys said, "Now the United States is in the war! Now it will end soon." Everybody was happy, they figured it was going to be a fast end.

I played soccer in the army. We stayed in a small town, Melrose, in Scotland–I still get letters from people I knew in that town–and they didn't have enough men in the town to play–all their boys have been in the army–so they came along to us if we would lend a few boys, but tell nobody, so we put on Scotch uniforms and played for them. About five of us. We won most of the time–we had strong players, some of the Polish-French boys have been international players. I was very good, not professional, but very good.

I was in Headquarters in Melrose, head office of the division, on guard, and two boys came in. They have been Polish-French. They spoke perfectly French–French was mostly their language–some Polish but not so good, and some German, too. They were Polish descent (not Jewish)–one was called Lerr and one was Wilk (in Polish, a wolf)–I think maybe they have been fake names. They both speak, but they wouldn't talk. They didn't stay long in our regiment–about two and a half months. I used to be very good friends with them, we played checkers together, had a beer together, but they never said anything. "You know, Goldberg, if some night we disappear from here, remember we are going on a mission." That's what I had from them, and about two or three months after, they disappeared and I knew but what or where I didn't know. I found out after that they both belonged to a special regiment, frogmen. A submarine brings them down, they swim to shore, and they went in to Le Havre, they blow up German boats. But in the port there's a gate, with wires, under the water, the Germans close it up and they have to find a way out. One didn't find his way back. One survived.

When the war was just over, I walked in Picadilly Circus and a guy says to me, "Hey, Goldberg, don't you salute a captain?" I look around, and I says, "There's no law we got to salute everyone with stars, with stripes," and he said, "Don't you recognize me, Goldberg?" "Lerr, tell me, where have you been?" and he was telling me the story that he was a frogman. They have been from that district, they knew the whole port. (They took people to send that know where to go and what to do, to supervise other ones how to get in or get out.)

I had other friends in the army. Rotcztain was one–the Rotcztain family had one of the nicest kosher delicatessens in Warsaw. He was studying medicine in France–the Poles have made it so bad for Jews in medical schools, even so bad no Jews could go at all. So a lot of them that could afford went away to France to study medicine. Sikorski asked all of them in France who had been Polish citizens to join the Polish Army, and Rotcztain came in with some friends till the Germans came into there and took it over. They came to England after Dunquerque, and they wanted to be in Intelligence, but the British wouldn't take them, so they tried to do it on their own. They took a boat and went over the Channel and the British caught them and they had to go back into the regular Polish Army.

In Scotland we built barracks, and we have been practising–you see, in the Canadian, American, British Army, a boy comes in and he knew right away how to drive a car, how to take apart a car, and a jeep isn't so hard for him to learn either–we didn't have that, we had to learn all that. And we had a lot of boys who have been unalphabets *(English-Yiddish for illiterates),* too (not Jewish boys, other ones, Polish) had to teach them how to read and write, you had to teach everything from the ABC. When I came to Scotland the first thing they put me on–I have been in a tank regiment–was how to take apart this and that from top to the bottom, a jeep, a lorry, a machine gun, and go on a convoy. We were in the First Polish Armoured Division, with General Maczek. Daytime, at night, we went out on manoeuvres, we have been training. We had everything, sports, running, and at night sometimes, in the hills in Scotland–you don't know how bad it was–it doesn't rain but that mist is worse than a heavy rain, it goes through your bones. We come back, wet like hell, have to change the uniforms, and the next day, out again. It all took time to learn, to train.

We didn't have equipment, nobody would give to us, they didn't have, they had to give it to the boys in Africa, to fill up whatever they lost. We all had to use the same rifles–if you went on guard, they counted out all your ammunition and if you used some you had to make a report what you did. We stayed near the ocean, near where Rudolf Hess landed,[35] near Glasgow, to guard the coasts. Who knew what could happen with the Germans, with the boats–they had so many?

We didn't have enough troops to put in a division. You know how they filled up our regiment? from Rommel's Army, from Afrika Corps, they captured them in El Alamein, they got some of the Polish boys who have been taken by force to the German Army. They were from Silesia[36]–the Germans claimed that this Silesia is their land, so these boys living over there, born over there, the Germans said they are Germans, they had to go in the German army, but they are Polish. When the British took them to prison camp, they asked these boys if they would like to go to the Polish Army. A lot of them when they were captured they didn't know if they wanted to go into the Polish Army or not, but after when they find out there's so many Polish boys, Polish officers, a lot of them are willing to join the Allied Forces. That's how we filled up our regiment. It took time to take them in, they had to investigate the boys they took prisoner. They have been very fine, good soldiers. We had a lot of them filled up our ranks in the division, if not we couldn't go to the war at all, we wouldn't have enough men. Officers, yes, but not enough men.

There was one boy we got from Rommel's Army, he stood behind me on a parade. I was a Lance Corporal then and he said to someone in German, "Ein Jude ein Obergefreite?" *("A Jew a Lance Corporal?")*–I heard this–so I turned around and give him a smack in the face. Mine captain afterwards, when we have been at ease, said, "What happened over there?" And mine sergeant said, "This man said this and this and Goldberg didn't take it and give him a smack in the face," so the captain called us both over into his office. He said to the boy, "I'll tell you something–you from Rommel's Army–we going to a front line and I wouldn't give away mine twenty-three Jewish boys who are in our company for a whole regiment of Germans. These boys who'll never let me down, you folks who run . ..." He said, "You know what? I'll tell you the truth, I wouldn't give two Jewish soldiers for fifty Germans soldiers to defend our lines." He said, "If I hear once more," and he took out the gun, "I'll shoot you in cold blood in the battlefield." Never heard nothing more. And that's it.

Mine regiment was all Polish–Jewish and Catholic mixed, no problems. We had two rabbis in our regiment: one was Rabbi Meltzer, one was Rabbi Klepfisch–he writes now in the *Jewish Forward.*

Was there anti-semitism in the army? To tell you the truth, in some regiments, a lot of our boys have been guilty–takes two to tango. Some of them went on leave, they didn't come back on time, and the MPs started looking for them. That's not fair. In mine regiment, there were quite a few Jewish boys, we have been the best in the regiment. I volunteered for everything, I said, "I'll take the worst when it comes–I have to defeat the Germans"–and that's it. Nobody opened up a high word to me anyplace. On the front line, everybody was the same.

I'll never forget General Montgomery, what he said when he came to visit our troops when we had been at Aldershot. He said, "Boys, you go in action, you're going to meet steel against steel, but you don't have to be afraid. In Poland you fought horses against steel, the Germans have been prepared, they fooled the whole world that they don't have nothing. I was with the Eighth Army in Africa, and we fought against Rommel, and German soldiers are good soldiers but if they find out that you have weapons too, better weapons than they have, they are cowards on the battlefield, they run. The biggest cowards you have ever seen will be the German Wehrmacht and especially the SS. Right away they will say, 'Kamerad.' *('I give up.')*" We met the Germans, and it was true, and the biggest cowards have been the SS. I met them in Normandy and we closed in the Falaise Gap.[37]

Our division was attached to the Canadian Army, and there came a day we went away from Scotland and we went to Aldershot–this is where the Scottish give you the last rites with their pipes–and from there we went to Tilbury, and from there overseas, to France. They wanted to put us on the first ship but our General said, "No, I'm not putting on mine First Army Division, I have but one division. I can't put to Normandy the first days, we have no more troops, put on other ones." We went the second wave. We met a boy on the boat took us down to a cabin, he was in the Polish Army in Windsor but his parents were American and we had a little party.

In battle I wasn't scared–I wanted to see the German cowards defeated–we just kept on going, even after Americans bombed our lines in Normandy. The Canadians couldn't get in contact with the Americans and we moved over to where the Germans have been, and the Americans bombed us and we lost a lot of men, a lot of artillery. It wasn't the Americans' fault. It happens.

General Sikorski was one of the finest men–he set up the Polish Government in Paris after the Germans took Poland. They have been afraid that he would organize European countries right after the war to go against Russia, he was killed in a plane with his daughter–not by accident. July 1943 he was killed. They picked a lot of soldiers to go to his funeral, but I didn't get to go. He's buried in England in the Polish Airmen's Cemetery in Nottingham.

CHAPTER XIII

We fight in France

"I took a little bit of calvados in mine helmet,
I stuck in the helmet mine feet–this stuff was
strong like hell!–to take off the sweat,
and I washed mine face from the dust."

Editor's note: K. Jamar, who served with the 1st Polish Armoured Division, in which Chaim Goldberg served, writes in detail of the Polish forces from their landing in Normandy to the surrender of the Germans to the British and the Polish Army at Wilhelmshaven in his book, With the Tanks of the Ist Polish Armoured Division. Chaim Goldberg's one goal was the defeat of the Germans. He was seldom concerned which ruined town was being fought over, and was more interested in his friends and fellow soldiers and how they fared.

We went into France, in Normandy, in July after D-Day. We became part of the Canadian Army now. The first week in August, it was very hot, we had to smash the German defenses on the road to Caen, open the road to Falaise. We had orders to hold every bit of land what we can hold and to not destroy any French homes or barns or cattle on account the people lost everything, to try to save that. And we did that, we tried to save, you know. Our general, Maczek, give the orders, the officers give us the orders–that was Polish orders, but maybe other ones, Canadians, English, Americans, got too the same orders from the head office. I never touched nothing in France–first of all they told us, "Don't touch nothing, you know, there's booby traps, you can touch something decent and it will blow you up in pieces," and that happened. I have seen mineself a lot of the boys touch something and it went like nothing, together with them. For instance, we had strict orders not to accept any flowers from any French people–they have thrown flowers with a hand grenade and a boy who was there was smart and he threw it back and killed some of them. In France, we fought in a village, and there was a little baby hanging on the wall, was marked in the German language, "For the blood of German soldiers who got killed in this village." But the Germans hanged it up as a trap, if you try to take it, you are going to get blowed up. I saw that with mine own eyes.

I never touched nothing–I have seen a lot of jewelry laying, I have seen all kinds of stuff laying around. But do you know what I took sometimes? It was so hot in France, I was so thirsty, and I have seen in jars pears, or some fruit, but I left the jar–*I did not destroy the jar.* This was in houses which have been mostly destroyed, only a little bit left here and there.

I don't like the French—the hell with them! I hate the French till today. I was on patrol in France, with a boy, Stefan Szymanowski—he was from France, he was born there, Polish descent. The whole company lost contact with the Germans—the worst thing you can do in a war is to lose contact with the enemy!—and mine captain sent me and Stefan and a boy named Nowak to find them. We took a jeep and went down, parked the jeep, looked around. Here comes a Frenchman, says something in French, and I says to Szymanowski, "What does he say?" and Szymanowski says, "He says there's no Germans here, the Germans are not around." I am suspicious, I don't believe, so we took him with us in the jeep. I said, "Here, take a helmet and stick it out on a stake near the jeep." When we hanged out that helmet we get a salvo from machine guns!—they have been right there like a close stick. I called mine captain right away on the radio and I tell him we found the enemy, and he says, "Start giving them fire!" That Frenchman—we took him with us, and turned him over to the Maquis *(part of the French Resistance)*, they've been looking for that man for a long time, but we didn't stay and wait to see what they're going to do with him. In every corner, in France, I didn't believe the French at all, and I don't trust them. French! some of them been Nazis![38]

After the war I was on leave in England and went back to France to go to mine regiment in Germany. You had to wait till ten o'clock at night to get a train back to Germany. I was walking with Stefan, and a French gendarme said a dirty word about the Polish—mine friend translated—and I give him a smack in the face and he took out a gun. I could handle mineself in those days so I took away the gun and we ran off. About four gendarmes came down to the station where we waited for the train to search for who did it, but couldn't find me: I took a pair of glasses from somebody, made mineself a black mustache, he couldn't recognize nobody and the train left. We had fought the Germans and lost men like nothing, and the French give up right away, and he says dirty things about the Poles!

We headed to Caen, to open the road to Falaise. Caen was ruined, bombed out. We passed Renemesnil, ahead was Soignolles, in front of us is Hill 111, we have to take that. We lose tanks and men and can't take the hill, the whole company moved out, moved back to Soignolles. I had a friend, Morris Lifshitz, and I asked mine captain on the radio, "Is Morris with you?" Mine captain says, "Goldberg, I think you'll have to go and bring back Morris," and I says, "I can't take alone," and a boy, a medic with the Red Cross on his arm, came with me. Morris got wounded, got hit in both heels, and he was laying over there. We went down, and I got 36 bullets in mine jeep delivering him—that's why they decorated me—he had the code for the British Army—if the Germans caught him!—you know every twenty-four hours there was a different code number to change the kilocycles on the radio—Morris was looking after it, he was the radioman—he got the code number from headquarters, special delivered. When I got to him I said, "Morris, tell me, what did you do with the code?" He says, "Hy, I teared them up in little pieces of paper and I swallowed them—so they couldn't find."

He was hurt in both heels, and I put him on a stretcher and in the jeep. You know, some jeeps have been specially equipped for four-five wounded men–mine jeep was equipped like that. We took off, made a lot of dust. I kept moving. I was sitting in the jeep down on the floor and driving, zigzagging around–with one hand I was steering and the other hand I keeped on the pedal. The Germans have been shooting but didn't get me. The boy with the Red Cross was next to me on the floor, I could just see over–the window was left down so a piece of glass wouldn't hit our eyes. I got Morris out and mine captain says, "Goldberg, did you find out what happened to the code?" and I told him, "He eat it up."

I took Morris down to First Aid, and there was Dr. Courland, very fine young man. I says, "Doc, what should I do now?" He says, "I can do nothing, he lost a lot of blood." He opened up the shirt, looked what kind of blood he needed to give him a transfusion and he says, "Take him down to the Second Aid, there's a plane takes him right out," and I came to the airplane. Here are white lines: if you go over the line is mines. The Royal Engineers digged out the road, throwed away the mines in the middle, and put on the white lines. I said, "Morris, give me your belt." He had in the belt all kinds of money, and I said to him "Give me the watch, give me the ring, I'll give it to the captain, he will send it out, and don't be afraid." Morris says, "Hy, here is mine ring," and he give me his ring, he give me his watch, his money which is soggy from perspiration, and I said, "Morris, God go with you." (He still has that same watch and that same ring–it's chipped a little bit from shrapnel, the ring, but he still has it.)

I give him a drink of water and he left. I give mine captain all his belongings. When Morris went to the hospital in England, English doctors wanted to cut off his feet. A Polish doctor said, "He's our soldier, a man without feet can't make a decent living," and a Jewish doctor said the same, "No dice! we are going to look after him." They patched him around, now he walks, dances, everything. (In fact, I got regards from Morris Linten, architect–he changed his name–he's still working, must be in his 80's. He's in Arizona.)

I was going back with the jeep and I had two flat tires from bullets and where can I go with two flat tires? I take out mine field glasses, and look around, there's a jeep laying over there in the field, tipped upside down. I said, "Listen, buddy, take off that Red Cross, you hold on to that machine gun, I'll take a couple wrenches with me." I walked down about a hundred yards, and I've seen there's nothing around–nobody got killed or anything–just happened that some boys tipped over that jeep–didn't want to give it over to the Germans or something. I took off two tires, and I took off the bad tires from mine–carried two tires just like that!–I was strong like a bull in those days!–and put on one tire and the spare had a bullet so I throw it away–why carry them?

There was a house there, a part of a house. And I said to the medic boy, "Listen, we are going to see inside." The cattle are running around, and goats and this and that, and the milk is running from them. I walked in that house, nobody was there, nobody, and there were standing big barrels of calvados–they made cognac from that. I went in and I took off mine shoes–I got in mine pack a new pair of socks, and I took a little bit of calvados in mine helmet–I stuck in the helmet mine feet–this stuff was strong like hell!–to take off the sweat, and I washed mine face from the dust. I said, "Wash yourself, too, Red Cross man!" and he did. I had water in mine jerrycan, and I spilled this out and I filled it up with calvados.

I came back and I've seen our Dr. Courland and I says, "Doc, I've got something for you" and he said, "What you got, Goldberg?" I says, "I find calvados, if you want a little bit," and he says, "Let me test it." So he tested it–and he said, "I want a can for mineself, too," so I give him some. I says, "Don't be shy, if anybody's wounded, give him a drop of that and he will go right to heaven!"

You know Dr. Courland had a banjo and played all kinds of songs. I can never forget how he sat with that banjo and played whatever you want–if you want a Polish waltz, he did it for you, if you want a tango, he did a tango, he was full of pep, you know, happy-go-lucky. He was a good doctor for the boys.

I had a second lieutenant, his name was Glassman–after became head chemist of Marks and Spencers in England. In Normandy he was wounded in the back at night–who did it, who made an attack, at night when you shoot you never know, you can't accuse this one or that one. People–a lot of them get excited! I heard on the radio that Glassman is badly wounded. Mine captain says, "Goldberg, you'll take him down to the First Aid." I took with me another medic boy with the Red Cross and I says to him, "You give me a hand." It was dark, I couldn't see Glassman, the boy found him, "He's laying here, he's wounded in the back, he's badly wounded." I came down to that Doctor Courland–he says, "Have any schnapps, Hy?" I says, "I think mine bottle is empty already." "But do you have any?" I says, "I think I got a drop cognac." He put him over upside down on the stomach in mine jeep. I drove with mine medic friend and the First Aid, they took him.

I never heard from him, never at all, but I knew he was alive. The war was over. Going to Israel the first time, I went to Scotland first to see friends, then came to London, and I looked in the phone book and found Ismar Glassman. He says, "Are you in London?" He called in about twenty boys, all Polish Jews from the Army–a lot of the boys stayed in England, lived just outside London. We had a big party and stayed talking till four o'clock in the morning. Some of the Polish boys from the Army have gone back to Poland but not the Jewish boys, there was nothing left for them to go back to. If Jewish boys went back to Poland it was not to stay–some of the boys have gone to find family but came back, went to Israel. Poland was no place for Jews any more.

One boy at the party given by Glassman–his name was Goldstein–and I says to him, "You supposed to be dead!" "What do you mean, Goldberg, I'm supposed to be dead?" "Are you really Goldstein?" He says, "Yeah! I'm really Goldstein!" When we were still in England, we couldn't go ten miles away from the barracks without permission and mine captain says, "Goldberg, you going ten miles from here for Passover night–there are special arrangements been made, an empty school, they give you the kitchen, take the truck." I told Goldstein, "We going for a Seder tonight." He says, "The hell with you, I'm not going." And he give me such dirty words and he didn't go. I told him, "Goldstein, you believe nothing but I'm just telling you, you going to be the first hit, and you're an old soldier"—he'd finished two and half years' service in Poland—everybody had to do it when you are nineteen—"when we land someplace wherever we're going to go, you are going to be the first gipporah hindel." (Years ago in mine childhood, on Yom Kippur, they used to buy a chicken and kill that chicken, a special rabbi did it, and that's the gipporah hindel, a sacrificial chicken, and you eat the chicken. You say to the chicken, "Me to life, you to death." But we don't do it any more, now you put in the basket some money, it goes away for charity—that's the gipporah hindel now.) He says, "I'm not going," and I says, "You don't have to go but you will see."

Do you know, in France, the German artillery was laying down fire and I heard on the radio this boy Goldstein was sitting in a German bunker what we'd taken over and the shrapnel went from over there and hit him first, badly—he was the first that got wounded in Normandy. It just happened! and I when heard on the radio that Goldstein is very badly wounded, I says, "Do you know what, Captain? I'm going to jump down, leave somebody to take over the radio." And I went down over there and Goldstein was half dead, the flesh was hanging down from the hips and the arms and everything. I took mine bandages and other boys' bandages, took a shirt, I teared it up, put it on him, and the artillery was laying such a fire that you have never seen in your life. I put him on mine shoulders and I carry down to a First Aid—there were a few priests and a few boys and doctors and I left him there, and two days after that I read in the order that Private Goldstein died from the wounds. That was the biggest shock when I have seen Goldstein at that party they made for me. He says, "You know, Goldberg, you tell me I'm going to be the first gipporah hindel and you have been the man who helped me. You bandaged me around, carried me on your shoulders, that's all I remember, nothing else." And till that day I didn't see him. He was alive! You know, so many got mixed up, so many tags.

In our company there were gangsters—we called them that in the army!—one was a gambler, named Stern, he would sell away the gun with the ammunition if he could get a few shillings to play in a poker game. He's the only boy I never have seen since the war finished. He had been going for a doctor in France. He was a 2nd lieutenant—a gangster I'm telling you, a gambler, in fact he owes me ten or fifteen pounds—maybe forty! I give him the money—you know why?—he gambled and he lost and he had to give it back to the boys.

When Stern was on patrol in Normandy, he and another two boys got in a place where there was a bunker with over one hundred SS men sleeping. Two German boys were guarding—one boy was sitting outside the bunker—they had two entrances—he fall asleep and Stern got in and they choked that German boy first and after they got the other one. The other German boy was writing a letter to his parents that he would like go to prisoners-of-war camp, can't take the war any more–we found the letter after. Stern with a few boys killed the Germans–some of them have been just wounded maybe–he made a massacre of them SS. (When they was going out from there one of our boys got on a mine and came up in pieces, just his tags left.) English soldiers find over there a wallet with a British licence, and the name was Stern, and they knew who it was who killed all those Germans. Montgomery decorated him himself.

Remember the boy from Rommel's army, the one I smacked? In Normandy before we closed in the Falaise Gap he broke his ankle and he couldn't walk. We couldn't go this way, nor that way, we had an order to hold on, not to let the Germans through–the German Army has to be destroyed and we must destroy that army there and then. I said, "Listen, don't worry, I'm going to fix your leg and you'll come out like a new man." I put him on the ground, straightened up his leg, took two sticks, took a shirt and teared it up in small pieces, and bandaged him around. I took his rifle, took out the magazine, threw it away, put the rifle upside down and took away his tags–maybe the German Army would find out his name or something, that he went from the German Army to us–and I hide it in mine pocket, and put the helmet on top of the rifle and I give him mine rations. I said, "Listen, here is mine chocolate,"–we had in cans chocolate–you could take one piece and you didn't have to eat a whole day!– "if you're hungry you'll eat it and here's some aspirins." I had some scotch and I give the boy what I had. The Germans didn't even bother, they just kept running wherever they could without their equipment, they left everything. They saw the helmet and just left him, they think they've seen a dead soldier and they have to run, what are they going to do? When we destroyed that German Army from the Falaise Gap, the medics came around and picked him up, took him away to First Aid and they just put him in a cast and that's it. He landed up in England, and I didn't see him after that. When he came back to the regiment I wasn't there any more, I was on the way to Canada. When the war was over a leather briefcase he sent me. I still have it–I offered it to my son the lawyer but he said it's too beautiful, so my grandson Noah will get it!

Chapter XIV

We fight in Holland and Belgium

Oct. 6th: "Polish losses severe."

At St. Omer, September 4th, 1944, we did a big job on the Germans, went into Belgium. From over there we went to Ypres, in fact I still have a camera I took off from a Hauptmann, a captain from the German Army. I stayed on guard, me, the boy Nowak, and another boy. A German captain was taking his wife to the station. He had a three-wheeler motor bike. Their motorcycles used to make a noise, tt tt tt, just like that. Ours was different–just like their guns and ours sounded different–you could recognize the difference on the front line–ours was sounding like a duck walking around–look, I tell you the truth! I says, "Ausweis!" *("Identification papers!")*–I studied German in school, speak it pretty well–and he says to me, "Ich bin Hauptmann these and these, War Office," he couldn't figure out if I'm on his side–he couldn't see in the dark. I says, "Where are you going?" he says, "I'm going to take mine wife to the station." We say, "You are a prisoner of war–the whole station is occupied." He was going to grab his gun and I says, "Wait a minute." We searched him, we took away a hundred and fifty American dollars, and I says, "Herr Hauptmann, where did you get dollars?" "Oh, we got from prisoners, American prisoners." I says, "American prisoners, it's no good for you, you can't keep that." We took him off, we took the motor bike, I took from him a beautiful pair of field glasses, which I still have, the other boys took, too.

There was a priest there. We told the lady, "You can go. Here is a priest, he'll take care of you." I told the priest, "Look, father, you take this motorcycle with you, take for yourself, don't give it away, take off the numbers and everything and it's yours. Look after this lady, take her to the Red Cross, we haven't got enough time to bother, she can take all her belongings." The Captain thanked us and I says, "Captain, the Krieg is over, for you, not for other ones." He says, "Unmögleich." (Unmögleich, means impossible.) They took him away, I didn't see him any more. I still have that wallet. I divided the money with the boys, American money, Belgian money, and we give some to the priest, we say, "Father, maybe you have to feed that woman, or something." We transferred the Hauptmann to our captain, and the German captain has told us they are trying to launch an attack on Roulers, they will win. We told him, but he didn't believe, the whole German army is kaput, and we took Roulers.

Jewish High Holidays we have been in Holland, and in the middle of the service came an order, "All men from the 9th Infantry Battalion come downstairs." And we got orders to go back to the battlefield and we went back about four, five o'clock in the morning. We had a jeep and I asked the captain, "Where are we going now?" and the captain says, "I don't know, nothing is delivered yet"–orders had to be delivered by a motor bike, special man delivers the messages–and after we find out we are going to liberate the Port of Antwerp and we liberated.

We had 140-150 prisoners from there, something like that–and mine captain give an order in the German language, every nationality to step out separate. Two Polish boys stepped out and we questioned them, and they said, "Some here is SS, they changed their uniforms at night and put in the ground somewhere." (These two Polish boys went to prisoner-of-war camp, they were from Rommel's Army, the SS also filled in their regiments from there as we did when we could.) Others step out: Lithuanians, Latvians, Estonians, Ukrainians, Austrians. Mine captains said to the SS, "We are not going to waste any ammunition on you. We had enough from you in Poland. You can go down to the water, and when the dike comes back, you can go for a swim." Whoever didn't have the tattoo from the SS–under the arm–they were prisoners of war. About 15, 20 were SS. They went with their captain, he shouted, "International law says you can't do that to prisoners," and we told him, "You are not prisoners, the Wehrmacht are prisoners, you have no right to change uniforms from SS to Wehrmacht, and Poland has suffered enough from you SS already." What happened to them I don't know.

We came back and it was a fast day, Yom Kippur, and we haven't eaten all day, and the captain says, "You going to eat now?" "No, the stars are not out. (The Sabbath is not over until three stars can be seen in the sky.) I need something to baptize the end of the fast!" "If you want I got a bottle of Scotch, something is better than nothing!" After came down the Sergeant and says, "Goldberg, I got a parcel for you." "I hope it's a good one, not a bomb inside." I told one of mine boys, "Open up, and we'll see." The parcel came from Herb Gray's mother[39], there was cookies, all kinds of chocolates and cheese, whatever you want was there. I took the package and give it to mine Sergeant Dupla and I said, "Divide it." (Dupla lived in Poland after, his son lived in Chicago, and on the Fourth of July Dupla was coming to see me, and on the railroad station platform he put down his briefcase and had a heart attack and died.)

Before we took Roulers, we went in a place called Wingeneh. The people from the town brought down all kinds of drinks and we had a few and mine lieutenant says, "Goldberg, where you going to stay tonight?" I says, "I'm driving up there on the cemetery with mine jeep and I'll curl mineself up, and devils can come to bother me!" I was supposed to get on the radio 5:30 in the morning but I slept in and didn't go on–they figured the Germans got me! Then I got on the radio, and mine captain says, "What happened?" I says, "I couldn't catch the station!" It was a big bluff, you know, and that was Wingeneh! I wasn't afraid of anything! if I die, I die, I was a single man.

We took a whole German army in Roulers, right where the Canadians fought in the last war, near Ypres. Leo Chertok–he was another one studying medicine in France when he came to the army–Leo spoke perfectly German, French, Polish, English. He said in German to the prisoners, "I want a parade here and all the German Army has to sing 'Wir Fahren Gegen Engelland'!" "Wir Fahren Gegen Engelland" *("We March Against England")*–this was their song. They made that whole parade, they sung that song marching off to prison–Leo Chertok had given them the command in German. I'm telling you! marching just like a parade, and that near Ypres. It made us so happy to see them like that!

We liberated a town in Belgium called Ghent, and a lady came out of a house and said to me in German, "Sind Sie ein Jude?" "Jahwol." "I've seen you have here Poland on your uniform." "I belong to that regiment." "I have here a Jewish doctor, he's from Germany, we hide him–he's from the *St. Louis* boat.[40] This is one of the men who jumped from the boat." We said, "You can tell the man to come out, not to be afraid." He came out and we said, "Listen, the war is over, you don't have to be afraid any more." He asked me for few pieces of soap–I give two bars, I give him corned beef a few cans, I give the lady something for hiding him out. We are moving, we had to capture a bridge before the Germans blow it up. He give me a white gold ring, two diamonds in both sides, in the top a pearl. I said, "I don't need anything." He said, "Take it." I give it to mine wife Ruth and she still has it.

The end of September, Tilburg and s'Hertogenbosch, we just went through; Barlanase–was a very big fight–we had a kick in the pants from the Germans, they let down fire, and we fight hard and the Germans give up the battle, and we kept on moving. Before we came to Breda we had to stay over there in Alphen for a while to straighten up the line–the British they went for a cup of tea!–we had an order not to destroy anything in Breda, infantry should go house to house.

We liberated Breda, we fought house-to-house there–they teached you how to look after yourself, and we have been told to watch ourselves, there can be a lot of Dutch SS who have been in the German Army,[41] keep an eye, one boy watch the other one, don't make too big of a movement. We took Breda without destroying the city and that's why we have been decorated in Holland, and for the liberation of Belgium we got like a rope around the shoulders. We got a Croix de Guerre, a special one–I am going to give it to mine grandson but I have so many grandboys I don't know who to give it to! But in Holland I was so careful I wouldn't touch nothing, I didn't want anything, I wouldn't drink the water, had enough food, they had a lot of Nazis in Holland. You know I didn't trust the Dutchmen–too many have been Nazis, like the French. You never knew who was a friend, who wasn't.

A couple of boys had been wounded and mine lieutenant had to go to take them down to Breda to hospital–we can't help them here at all, and it's dark like hell. I didn't feel like going but I said to mine boy from the Red Cross, "Listen, you drive and I'll walk and I'll show you." We had phosphor sticks, and I showed him. We got away from the German fire and took the boys down to Breda and went back to the bridge over the Maas River, over where we stopped for the winter.

In Breda, mine captain says, "Goldberg, it's for Christmas night, maybe we can get some fish?" He have seen me many times with a fishing rod, with a worm–I have always looked in the water to see what's there. I hadn't got with what to get any fish but I said, "Give me a few hand grenades and a little boat, I'll go out and I'll get." You throw a couple of hand grenades into the water and it blows up and the fish come up. I got lots of fish, white bass. I prepared the fish and everything. (I could cook anything! anytime! anyplace!) At night came an alarm: we had to go out to the line and I've never seen the fish, and I didn't get back–other people ate it!

Christmas night Leo Chertok was controlling the artillery. He was in a special post–whenever an enemy truck went by, he give them fire. The Germans started to fire back onto our side. I had a second lieutenant, Elvar Shotski–he was a wrestler. We had been dressed in white uniforms for the snow and the Germans tried to land, they have wanted to cut through the lines and about eight Germans and the lieutenant landed from the water a few hundred feet from us. Elvar Shotski tapped someone to give the signal and down the line one give the other one the tap–the signal–we didn't have to talk to each other–open up fire–three of the Germans got killed, a couple got wounded and the rest lift up the hands, they surrendered. The first thing their lieutenant asked, "What kind of day is today?" and we answered, "Weinachten" *("Christmas").* He said to mine captain, "Herr Captain, spare me a cigarette," so the Captain took out cigarettes, and he asks if anybody has a shot of liquor and he says, "The Krieg *(war)* is for me over. Wir haben ihn verloren. *(We have lost it.)*"

The Germans send out a rocket from Holland going towards England and the rocket didn't take the course, it circled around and went down on the German headquarters, and a few hundred German soldiers got killed and wounded.[42] When we took German prisoners, they talked right away, where V-1 is, where V-2, they told, "This is the place they've been shooting from in Holland." And the Intelligence hold them not even for ten minutes! They mark down everything, and everything came very handy. I've seen a lot of them rockets, they went over our heads.

The 30th of December at Kapelshe Veer, we lost quite a few boys, and the Canadians, the British got in and took it. We tried, we couldn't take it, we couldn't do it. I have seen them British boys, commandos, they went with bayonets and knives, and them Germans have been afraid like nothing, the British took them out like rabbits from the ground. They took that island. But they did drink a lot of tea!

At New Year's Leo Chertok got hit, I hold him by the hand, and he give me his watch and says, "Goldberg, if you're going to live, give this away to mine family." He died on mine hand. So I keep that watch for later to give and one day I got hit and the watch fell apart–what am I going to do? nothing was left. He died in the winter and the Germans buried him, and when the ground got soft we went and dug him up–we had been afraid, the Germans just put the boys into shallow graves, they put mines in there. We made the funeral in Holland.

Leo was supposed to marry a girl in London. He didn't make it. Very fine boy.

January-February-March. We stayed in homes, in barracks, in schools, for the winter. April 18th we reached the Ems River, starting to fight again. We are getting close to the German border! We went on towards a place called Gogh—it was supposed to be the Siegfried Line[43], and I really wanted to see that Siegfried Line! We went through there, and it was nothing, just big pillars from cement that tanks couldn't go, they would break up in pieces. An old man with a white mustache was chasing around a sow with little pigs and the whole city was bombed out to hell and I says, "Sagen Sie 'mal, Kamerad, welche Stadt ist dies?" ("What city is this?") He says to me, "Es war einmal eine große Stadt, Gogh, sie ist nicht mehr." ("It was once a big city, Gogh, but it isn't any more.") And I looked at the map, and I think, "I know where I am." I got on the radio and I told mine captain, "There's nobody here, just a man chasing some pigs, stay where you are and don't move, the whole German company will come out, but keep an eye out for snipers." And we went down to the Siegfried Line and I said, "I have to do something!" I went down to the pillar, and the boys made a sign: "Goldberg scheiß an der Siegfried Line." I couldn't believe it! I look around, and right away there's a sign![44]

German soldiers have been going along to prison camps—nobody captured them or nothing, they have been coming towards us with their hands up. We told them, "Don't hide yourself, throw everything out, and you can go away to prisoner-of-war camp." There must have been about forty or fifty of them, they have seen that we are already in Germany, we are on the Siegfried Line—you know, like the Maginot Line—the Frenchmen fought like nothing, Feh! I've never seen them on the battlefield. (You know what the Czechs said? Before we went on to land in Normandy they were supposed to go with us. They said [in Czech; he translated] "We are not going to fight for the British marmalade what they give us!" That's what they said!)

In Holland our regiment moved—when this regiment goes this way, that one goes there, a pincer movement—our regiment moved a little too fast—the British played a soccer game, they had a cup of tea! (But the British have been good soldiers: British commandos, if they went on a job, they made that job well!) If we would go farther the Germans would circle us around, a regiment has to go all one length, and we had to wait for the British.

So while we waited till the British straightened up the front, two of our boys, Muzyczko and Stern—that gangster! have nothing to do, and they find out there's a jewelry store with a big safe there in Alphen, all deserted—the owners have run away. These boys built a wall with stones to protect themselves, and they put in an anti-tank gun and they opened up the safe like that, and they got out all kinds of stones from that safe, got out gold and diamonds and watches, whatever you want. Mine captain got a beautiful diamond ring, must be four carats—in England his wife just had a baby boy, and next day he was supposed to go to see his wife and the baby. Muzyczko and Stern wanted money to play cards! (That Muzyczko and that Stern! They had been wounded in Canal Mark, they had been waiting on a Bren carrier for the medics to pick them up. Stern's knee was hanging down and Muzyczko his shoulder the same thing and you know what they did? They played a poker game for the last few diamonds they had!)

We had been in Breda and from Breda we had to cross Canal Mark to get the Germans out. The Germans blew up the bridge–we could hear them over the other side, they couldn't hear us. We went early in the morning about 4:30-5:00, it was dark, we were supposed to capture that place across the river and move out the Germans. We got across, but there was such a fire from the Germans! I was laying there next to mine captain–we were laying all flat–and he was holding mine hand, and he says, "Goldberg, try to help me." I says, "Captain, I do the best what I can." And that's it, I have seen he's dead, and a lot of the boys were dead.

I said to mine Lieutenant Gorelik,[45] "He's dead, what shall we do?" and he says, "Goldberg, how much ammunition you got?" I said, "Two magazines and three hand grenades." And I had mine rifle and machine gun. He says, "You know how to swim?" I says, "Yes," and he says, "Look, either you go first in the water, and I'll support you, or I'll go first in the water, and you support me," and I decide I'll go first. It was dark, it was not far away, so I throw the hand grenades at the Germans in the dark–you didn't know where you throw them or what–and he kept supporting me with fire and I swimmed over and he swimmed over, back to our side. When I went in the water I have seen mine jacket was heavy–I had all kinds of souvenirs and stuff in that jacket–so I throwed it away.

(Someone who painted the house stole all my other souvenirs from the war, but one souvenir I still have: a double decoration SS from a Dutch SS man in Holland. I took it off from him, I teared off that SS decoration. You know what we did to him? We took him onto the third floor, and by the hands and feet we threw him out from the window. Honest to God. The people living below didn't believe, didn't know an SS man lived upstairs. Another time we were fighting hand-to-hand in Holland and there was a Dutch man changing into civilian clothes in a house and he said he wasn't SS but we find everything: the boots, the decoration in his wallet and the Dutch people finished him up.)

And that's it, we were in the water, it came all like a dream. I came back next day to find we lost forty-one men. Mine dead captain–the Germans had cut off his finger to get the diamond ring he had for his wife. We buried forty-one Polish boys there in Holland, in Breda.

(I went back to pay respects there after the war. I returned with mine wife Ruth, our twenty-fifth wedding anniversary. We have been in Holland, in Amsterdam. I says, "I am going down to the cemetery." I took the train–takes about an hour and a half–got a cab driver. I told him, "I am looking for the Polish Cemetery," and he showed me one, but I says, "That's not the one, I buried my friends near a church." And I find this guy lives across the street from it! All them boys in the cemetery, so many boys, he didn't know.)

Mine god, mine god, over there, the cemeteries, Canadian boys, Polish boys,

English boys, American boys. The graves haven't been even filled up yet, the Germans took out from them all kinds of stuff, robbing from the cemetery knives, rings, watches, whatever they could, they wanted to have souvenirs. The boys were buried but not so good, you couldn't always dig right, the ground wasn't–winter, I don't know. We tried never to leave our boys laying around in the battlefield dead. We took them with us when we could and a lot of times I put them on a jeep, but we couldn't always.

There was a boy Wislocky and he had four boys wounded on his jeep, and he was driving from the front line to the First Aid Station. I was behind him and a sniper shot that boy, and I've seen he lost control of that jeep. I stopped mine jeep and went down on the ground on all mine fours–I went down to shut off his ignition, you know, and the jeep came to a stop. Wislocky was dead already, we opened up fire against the Germans, and I took one hand grenade–I remember like now–and I watched and watched and I've seen that this German is lifting his head out of the tank and I just threw it right inside there and it blew him up and a few German boys start to run. And I hollered on the radio that somebody should take over this jeep–there's four boys wounded on this jeep. I took two of them, and there came up about ten Germans, they came out and they surrendered. The Germans said that they had been left special to hold back our regiment so not to let us go so fast ahead.

We kept on going, we landed in Mappin, we liberated a camp there and we found a few hundred Polish women soldiers in uniforms–the Germans captured them in Warsaw fighting, in the uprising.[46] I don't remember too much about it–so much going on, you know. We got in contact with families–in the United States, in Canada. I got in a shipment of packages–the British didn't like it and they wanted to put me in a court martial–they thought I was in the black market! Mine captain had to back me up. I told them, "I sent some letters to these people and give them mine address–and Dr. Courland's," and we give the women the things from the packages. And it was all right, but you know, a lot of boys have been dealing in the black market.

On the borders from Holland and Germany, we kept on going towards Wilhelmshaven, when I have seen the Canadians put on guns thicker than big trees. There were six staying in one spot firing one after the other. I said, "Boys, the war is over if the Germans see these guns." They fire from one, let it cool off, fire from another. You could see them Germans are starting to run all over. The big soldiers left, they put on young kids, they put on them a swastika, a uniform. I was near Pappenburg, I was driving a jeep, and I have seen young boys about sixteen walking. I have mine boy with the Red Cross with me and I have a jeep and I have a machine gun and I have a radio and I have everything, and I call mine captain and I say, "Captain, here are so many and I don't know how I can handle it." "Give them an order to lay down the weapon and stay there and the boys will give you a hand, don't take any for prisoners, don't shoot them, they're young boys, we've got orders not to bother with them."

Second Lieutenant Elvar Shotski–the wrestler–a husky boy, when he'd sit on that motor bike, he looked like a gangster from Chicago. The Germans have been afraid when he used to go through with his motor bike on the battlefield. These boys, some of them started to surrender, they didn't shoot at all. I have seen farmers, crying that they took the boys just out from the farm and the big shots ran away, they wanted the boys to defend them. We told them, "Listen, the war is over for you boys, you go home where you belong." They didn't even wear any uniforms. We searched them, they don't have anything, they have been running away and they give us their weapons. So we sent them home, young boys, twelve, fourteen, fifteen years old. They were around there in the Poppenburg/Oldenburg area.

Chapter XV

The War Ends

"We didn't need, we didn't want, we didn't take, German food."

We heard the surrender of the Germans on the radio. We waited for instructions, and we had parties, they give us all kinds food–we didn't need, we didn't want, we didn't take, German food. They dumped the water from the special water trucks and filled up with alcohol from a factory for that–right in Germany. After we went in to Wilhelmshaven for the surrender and there they give an order to the German crews–there was a lot of U-Boats stationed there–to surrender, put on white flags, the same size like we had in Poland! In Poland the Germans give out notices to put on this size flags so we made them use the same ones. We got one German who had marched on Warsaw, he couldn't believe, he couldn't *believe* we beat them! When the Germans came in Gdansk, there was a Polish eagle there and they took it off and they put it on in Wilhelmshaven. Now we give them an order to bring this down just like it was, to hand it over. We make the Germans make a big parade, the generals with the officers, with the soldiers, everything, and they surrendered to the Poles in Wilhelmshaven! I live for this day! My every dream is answered!

Three or four days after the war was over the medic boy I was with when I had a flat tire in Normandy–we couldn't find him, everybody says he deserted. I said, "Why should he desert now, the war is almost over?" We find him dead near a little creek, covered up with branches. SS men got him. Mine captain give an order: if they don't step out–them guys who killed that boy–we are going to destroy the whole village. "We are going to make like you made in Lidice, in Czechoslovakia, we are going to make you a Lidice right here, all you officers. Every tenth person is going to get shot."[47] Some girls said, "In that place is two German soldiers hiding." We got them, we give them over to another regiment, they went through a trial, they hanged them, and that's it. That's what happened to that boy from Poland with the Red Cross on his arm, lived all through the war. Why did they kill him? Just the SS, that's how they were. I was with him in France. He was a good boy, a good Polish boy. Every company has two of them boys with the Red Cross on their arm, their job was to help wounded boys, Americans called them medics. The Germans have been told they didn't hold any weapon.

And after that, no more fighting. Everybody started to look after the concentration camps, the people have been so sick there. The Jewish people didn't want to go back to Poland, so they bring them to the British zone. I was in the occupation forces for almost a year. I was stationed for that year around

Poppenburg, moved about five or six times. Was I afraid to walk in Germany? no, but I always carried with me a small gun in mine pocket–I never used it. If I needed something, if I wanted a role of film, I went down to a German photography store and said, "Listen, you have a role of film?" "I'll get it for you." "I'll come down tomorrow if you have one." We never asked for free. Sometimes you give a package of American cigarettes–I didn't smoke–some boys made fortunes from cigarettes. I didn't bother, I give away mine cigarette rations to mine friends in the service. The only thing what I used to buy is sometimes a bottle of Scotch for two packs of cigarettes. Polish people didn't go for Scotch, I didn't like anything else–mix with a little water, you don't get a headache. I had a bottle of champagne what I got in Normandy, I carry it back to Canada, and when we bought the house here in Windsor, we invited in a few people and opened it up–mine god, it was really strong!

They never give a credit to the Polish boys–the Canadians didn't give, the Americans didn't give, the British didn't give–but I tell you something, they sacrificed men like nothing. Polish boys were in the Royal Air Force, they fight in Italy, in Africa, give the British the Germans' code. And they got nothing after the war was over!

The British liberated Bergen-Belsen. We didn't know what had been going on, we didn't know till the last minute. The only thing I knew was a man by the name Arthur Ziegelbaum, from the Bund, they smuggled him out from Poland–he came and spoke in England, and he went even to the United States and told that they are burning people alive without any reason, not shot or nothing, just throwing them in gas chambers and they burn them in stacks, pour over them kerosene, they didn't have enough room in the gas chambers, and he was telling what was going on. And nobody believed. And he says, "Without Jewish people I haven't got what to come back to Poland." And he committed suicide, and that Ziegelbaum was coming from mine home town of Pulawy, he was a landsman from Pulawy.

I went with Dr. Courland to Bergen-Belsen right after liberation and he carried with him a big jug of rubbing alcohol. He said, "Wait, Goldberg, I'll pour over you that rubbing alcohol," just like that, over the uniform and everything and on mine hands and he said, "Don't touch nothing." (I don't know what happened to him–when I went into civilian life, he was still in the army.) In Bergen-Belsen there was laying there the dead people, thousands of carcasses, they made the Germans dig trenches to bury them–and not to throw. They give them an order right away, "No throwing!" but lay down flat the people to rest in peace. No others but Germans alone, some of them girls, SS, they didn't like to do it, and one of our boys went down and says, "Are you going to do it? this is you people, you did it." I still have mine pass to go into Bergen-Belsen.

In Bergen-Belsen I recognized the wife and sister of mine boss Mr. Argant, they have been laying over there, but they never recognized me. They had typhus. They have been dressed on the top with a bag from potatoes, and for a skirt, another bag from potatoes. Next day I brought some clothes, then I spoke to them and wrote a letter to a brother of one of them in Illinois. They sent me a picture maybe three-four months after. The Allied armies did everything: they brought down food and disinfectants and doctors and medicines, and whatever you want. A lot of soldiers didn't bother to take any ration so to give to the people, they did the best what they could. Whoever came to a concentration camp give away everything they had. Thousands of carcasses of people. So many people. I didn't go to any other camps.

CHAPTER XVI

After the War

"We didn't come to rob the German people, we liberated."

After the war I was sent for occupation to Louroup, on the border of Holland. The first day I walked in a house and asked the lady in a nice way in the German language if she has a room to spare for six boys. "If you haven't got it, we don't force you to give us, we didn't come to rob the German people, we liberated." She says she has. I told them mine name is Goldberg and I said, "Ich bin ein jude" [I am a Jew]. Her son Herman was so happy–he had been two years in a concentration camp. Not far from there was a camp for Jews from Holland and he had thrown food over the fence, and somebody squealed on him. He was a farmer, too old for the army, the only son.

At night, in the evening, we used to bring in our food to eat supper, and we had white bread, and I've seen the eyes of that old lady popping out for that white bread. I said to her son, "Herman, can you spare me a piece of black bread, I want to eat a piece–I'll give you the white bread, I would like the black bread." He says, "Sure, mine mother will be glad to give it to you," and she give me right away half a loaf of black bread, and took the white bread. I liked the black bread better, what I had eaten before in Poland.

This man Herman said to me, "Mr. Goldberg, I'll tell you something. Before the war in mine barn I kept a tank here, I had to sign for it. In every barn there was stationed a tank. Nobody had to know about it and that's all. The owner of the barn had to sign that he had a tank and that nobody's touching it." That man Herman is telling me, "Every four weeks came a crew, start up those tanks, drive out, look at the radio, everything works, came back, put it up, not covered up outside but inside the barn." Our Polish government didn't see what Germany is doing! The Germans have fooled the whole world, Chamberlain has been fooled. Nobody have seen how many they had, and that's it, that's how they prepared for war.

I was sitting with Herman late one night. Louroup was such a beautiful village, and I asked, "You have here any Jewish people?" He said, "You know most of the Jewish people have been in that other town over there, they handled the cattle and horses, very well-to-do people. The Nazis came and they took out to the concentration camp the Jewish people. There was one lady, not Jewish, she was married to a Jewish fellow, she give out her husband to the Gestapo. The Burgomeister didn't want them to take him, him and the boy–their son–but they went. She was left."

About three days after Herman told me that, that Jewish man and his son came back with Herman. His mother took them in and they made them some supper and I told them, "I am Jewish, too." They said they would like to go home, get a ride home, but after seven o'clock in the evening nobody has the right to be on the streets, there is a curfew, special patrols are staying on the roads and watching. So I called mine captain and I says, "Captain, I got here two survivors, Jewish people, they want to go home, they live not far away from here, you think you can give me passes? Can I take a jeep and take them down?" He said, "Go ahead," and I took them back over there. And the Burgomeister told the man who give his name out and the man found his wife and cut her head off. They arrested him, they took him to Poppenburg in Germany to go through a trial.

We still had in our regiment Max Rosenthal, he was a lawyer–he was after at the Nuremberg trial[48]–he was to defend this man. He went and told the man, "It looks bad." The Jewish Brigade–the army from Palestine, the ones who organized all those refugees and smuggled them into Palestine, and smuggled guns and ammunition–find out that they have on trial a man like that.[49] They fixed it that when that man walked out from the trial to the washroom, the Jewish Brigade boys put him in a jeep and they took him off and he never came back. He disappeared, I don't know where and what. The Jewish Brigade found out about this because they used to come around to buy weapons–they took them apart and smuggled the parts into Palestine, and we told them boys what was going on.

I asked the lady where I was staying, "Do you have anybody in the States"? She said, "I have a brother in Pennsylvania." He was a Catholic priest. I wrote him a few words, "I am stationed here, if you want to send something, send to me and I'll give it to them." (This was only a little bit after the war was finished, no packages could be sent direct.) I told the priest I wasn't staying here too long. Do you believe it didn't take more than three weeks a big package came! I opened up and inside was a letter for these people. They were so happy, Herman offered me anything. I said, "I don't need, I got enough food here." He says, "You don't know what it's worth to mine mother and me and mine sister that we find out that our uncle is alive." After I stayed over there three months–not even–I left that place. From Lourop we went to Poppenburg and Oldenburg.

In Bergen-Belsen I was talking to boys who have been liberated from there and they said, "We have a boy from your home town," and it was my cousin! Haskel Tanzman! from mine father's side. I give him some food, I give him mine cigarettes, he left to be smuggled into Palestine. I couldn't believe that he survived! I went to see him in Israel a couple of times. He has two boys and a girl. In 1967 he and his two boys have all been in the army, were ten kilometres away from Cairo.

I was in London after the 1967 war,[50] and I saw a colonel in the Israeli Army. He had been in the same Polish Army division with me, but was in communications. I looked at him, he looked at me, he says, "Goldberg, recognize me?" I says, "Tell me, where did you go from England?" He says, "I went to Israel, I left one war, went to another war!"

Postscript

I was demobbed 10 September, 1946. I applied to go back to Canada. Canada didn't want so many Jews but the boys who volunteered there, they had a chance.[51] Nobody survived of mine family–if anybody would be alive I would have gone back to Poland but everything was destroyed, nobody left.

I went down to the Canadian Consul.

Ruth Goldberg recalls: In the spring of 1946 we couldn't get a visa for Chaim to return to Canada. So my father Max Kander got in touch with Paul Martin Sr.–he knew him from the Depression days–and he got him the visa.

They sent me a letter they'll give me a visa if I'll find transportation to Canada. There were hundreds of people waiting to go to Canada. I had a friend, that Kleiner with the gold watch, and his brother was going out with a girl whose uncle was a big man in Cunard Lines. I said, "I'll treat you and your girlfriend and your brother and her uncle with a big dinner if you can get me a passage on a boat." He says to me, "Goldberg, I don't want money, I don't want nothing, why should you pay for me?" But I give him ten pounds just to have a good time, and I got a ticket–I paid fifty-one pounds (a lot of money then, the pound was at five American dollars)–and I came down to the Canadian Consulate in Trafalgar Square and the Consul said to me, "You're going to tell me that you got already passage to go back to Canada?" I said, "Sir, here I got the ticket already," and he said, "Men like you we need, just go inside and let the doctor check you up if you're fit for Canada and that's it!"

You never know what happens in life, you never know what's going to happen to you. I would never believe in mine life I'm going to come to Canada, the United States, England, Japan. I said to mineself, "I have to meet the German Army, see them defeated," and that was mine only dream.

I came back to Windsor the 11th of August, got married September 15, 1946. Mine son Jerry–named for mine father Judka–was born the next year, then Sydney–for mine brother Scholem–two years later, and then Allan–after mine grandfather Abram Yitshak–nine years after. I got mine brother Noah in one of Allan's boys. I have eleven grandchildren–all boys, only one girl. All mine sons are educated: Jerry is a lawyer, lives in Windsor; Sydney is a principal of a high school, in Toronto; Allan has a business degree, works in Detroit.

Endnotes

1 M. Laffan, "Weimar and Versailles: German Foreign Policy 1919-1933," in M. Laffan, ed. The Burden of German History 1919-1945 (London, 1988), p. 86, elisions in Laffan.

2 Louis L. Snyder, Historical Guide to World War II (Westport, Conn., Greenwood Press, 1982) from Documents on German Foreign Policy, 1918-1945. From the Archives of the German Foreign Ministry (H.M.S. London, 1948 ff.) D.VII, No. 193, p. 750.

3 In 1945, the American journalist I.F. Stone met a Polish Jew who had been evacuated to Russia; after the war she returned to Poland to see if she could find any relatives. She recalls, "The reception we got in Poland was not a pleasant one. The first thing we heard when the repatriates came across the Polish border from the USSR were cries of 'zhidi kommunisti' (Jew Communists). For those Poles we were only more Jews to kill. I don't ever want to see Poland again." Stone met a Polish Jew who had fought against the Germans for five years; he returned to his native land as a soldier in the Polish Army and helped to liberate Warsaw. "'And do you know the reception I got?' he asked me in Yiddish. 'I meet a Polish woman and she says to me ... I, who am a soldier in Polish uniform, mind you, and she knew I was a Jew ... to me she said, 'The one bad thing about Hitler is that he didn't kill all the Jews.' 'Do you think I wanted to stay in Poland after that?'" Underground to Palestine (New York: Boni & Gaer, 1946), pp. 76, 51 and see also pp. 16-17, 49-52.

4 Pulawy was a small city of about 6,000, on the Vistula River in the Lublin District, about 120 kilometres from Warsaw; it was approximately half Jewish.

5 The issue of Sunday opening had been contentious since the end of the nineteenth century. In England and the United States the day-of-rest question was social and religious, but in Poland it was political and "racial," i.e., Jewish, since Jews were the only ones whose holy day was Saturday and who therefore worked on Sunday.

6 The historian Lucy S. Dawidowicz spent 1938-9 in Vilna (then part of Poland) and wrote, "In 1936, Poland was an even more degrading place for Jews to live than Hitler's Germany. The 3,300,000 Polish Jews had been forced into poverty and deprived of opportunity by the economic policies of the Polish authorities. Outbreaks of anti-Jewish violence had recently spread across the country, in several places taking on the proportions of full-blown pogroms." By the late 1930s, the "don't-buy-Jewish" boycott had developed into a nationwide movement. The Polish politician Roman Dmowski had begun the boycott movement in 1912 to punish the Jews for having helped defeat his party, the Endecja.

In September 1935 the Nuremberg Laws passed by the Nazi government deliberately created "a barrier between Jews and non-Jews that existed nowhere else in the modern world. Marriages between Jews and non-Jews were forbidden; extramarital relations between Jews and non-Jews were forbidden; nor could Jews employ any non-Jewish German women under the aged of forty-five. In a series of thirteen specific regulations following on the Nuremberg Laws, Jews were barred from all official and professional life in Germany. ... Neither quality of past service, nor respected position in society; neither ability nor age, could protect a Jew in Nazi Germany." Martin Gilbert, Exile and Return: The Emergence of Jewish Statehood (London: Weidenfeld and Nicolson, 1978), pp. 162-3.

Polish trade and professional associations learned from the Germans to introduce an "Aryan" requirement into their bylaws, excluding Jews from membership and from practising their trade or profession. Endecja called for "the de-Judaizing of Poland" and for "propaganda on behalf of Polish commerce and handicraft." Gentile merchants' and artisans' associations pressured city governments to keep Jews from participating in trade fairs, deny them licenses to practise certain trades, and limit their number in various occupations. Dawidowicz, From that Place and Time, p. 172.

7 The Polish Falanga was named after the Falange, the Spanish Fascist organization; it had considerable following among Polish students, one of whose major activities was organizing anti-Jewish riots and assaulting Jews.

8 The government-run Polish universities promoted numerus clausus *(quotas for Jews)* and from

1921 to 1939 the number of Jewish students in Polish universities declined from 24.6 percent to 8.2 percent. The idea of "ghetto benches"–special seats for Jews in university classrooms–was passed by the Seym *(Parliament)* in 1937. Jewish students refused to use the benches and stood through the lectures. The Wawelberg Technical High school in Warsaw, founded by two Jewish industrialists in 1901 with the understanding that Jews would not be subject to discrimination there, was the first college to expel a Jewish student for not using a ghetto bench. But a numerus clausus was not enough for the Endecja, which agitated for a numerus nullus, no Jews at all in the universities.

9 The meat trade was almost entirely in Jewish hands and therefore the meat sold had been ritually slaughtered. While the grounds for the law were supposedly humanitarian, the real purpose was to reduce the number of Jewish butchers, which it did.

10 But it was not fake, though Chaim Goldberg could not know that: the English newspaperwoman Clare Hollingworth wrote that news was simply not verifiable.

11 One of the major German extermination camps. Anne Frank and her sister Margot died there in 1945. When the British entered the camp April 15, 1945, there were 30,000 inmates.

12 Vilna, a centre of Jewish life for hundreds of years, was the ancient capital of Lithuania. The Poles seized the city after World War I, when the country became independent again. After World War II, Lucy Dawidowicz wrote, "Vilna no longer exists. On its site stands a place identified on the map as Vilnius, capital of Lithuania ... the Vilna described in Jewish annals now lies buried beneath the debris of history, beneath layers of death and destruction. When the Soviets first occupied Vilna in 1940, they Sovietized it, destroying its historic identity and its Jewish particularity. The Germans who followed destroyed Vilna altogether, murdering nearly all of its 60,000 Jews–men, women, and children. ... A visitor to today's Vilnius can no longer find a trace of what had once been the Jerusalem of Lithuania. ..." From that Place and Time, p. xiii.

13 When Russian soldiers invaded Poland, "Shopkeepers told strange stories of the superstitious awe with which their new customers regarded even the most ordinary commodities: much they had never seen before and did not know its use ... grown men clutched at novelties, broke them and discarded them. Watches they prized above all else, army officers pinning two and three at a time on their tunics like decorations: what most astonished them was the ticking, until Red commissars felt moved to explain that watches which worked were merely an insidious form of bourgeois propaganda." Lilian T. Mowrer, Arrest and Exile: The True Story of an American Woman in Poland and Siberia 1940-41 (New York: Morrow, 1941), pp. 24-5.

14 Olga Kochanska (a Polish-American who had married a Pole) was arrested by the Soviets and with many others was put into a locked cattle car without no food, water, or toilet facilities. They were given no explanation as to why anyone had been arrested or where they were being sent. Suddenly the door was "thrown open and a Russian guard appeared in the aperture ... an elderly woman angrily demanded that they be allowed to get out and buy something to drink. "'Why should we suffer so?' she protested vehemently. He looked at her apathetically. "'Suffer?' he repeated, 'Why should you not suffer? We have been suffering so for twenty-two years.'" Mowrer, Arrest and Exile, p. 34.

15 The consul was Senpo Sugihara. "He did this, by all accounts, out of moral conviction, without official sanction or permission from his superiors. Even as he was being transferred by the Japanese government to another post in war-torn Europe, Consul Sugihara was issuing transit visas on his way to the railroad station, and even in the railroad car before the train began moving. ... He is the only Japanese honoured with a tree and a plaque on the Avenue of the Righteous Gentiles in Yad Vashem in Jerusalem, and ... one of his sons and a grandson live and work part of each year in Israel." Esther Hautzig, Remember Who You Are: Stories About Being Jewish (New York: Crown Publishers, Inc., 1990), p. 91.

When the Foreign Minister in Tokyo learned what Sugihara was doing, he was ordered to leave, which he did on September 1, 1940. "During the past nineteen days, he had stamped and signed nearly six thousand visas entitling their bearers to remain in Japan for a maximum of twenty-one days while in transit between any two countries. Whether Tokyo would honor the visas, he did not know." Marvin Tokayer and Mary Swartz, The Fugu Plan: The Untold Story of the Japanese and the Jews During World War II (New York & London: Paddington Press Ltd, 1979), p. 80.

16 The NKVD, Stalin's secret police, was a continuation of the Communist OGPU, a successor to the Tsarist secret police. Later acronyms were MGB and KGB.

17 To Polish-Jewish refugees the trip was an extended exercise in anxiety and anticipation. "There was nothing, absolutely nothing, to prevent the Russians from marching onto the train, culling them out from among the other passengers and taking them off to be shot. There was no basis for hope that they would not be pulled off the train at any of the Siberian stops and marched to a labor camp, there to spend the brief remainder of their lives. With every mile that passed, the refugees were going deeper and deeper into enemy territory." Tokayer and Swartz, The Fugu Plan, p. 107.

18 Olga Kochanska wrote of a prison in Kazakstan to which Poles were sent. A fifteen-year old girl had written to her aunt: "We live in a hole in the ground. It is quite a large hole, and wooden poles support the turf walls which are covered with dry clay and manure. We have a stove but it fills our hole with smoke. Yesterday two of us fainted. Our ceiling is so low that we can touch it with our hands and we have to crawl to go in and out. We are sometimes shaken with laughter at the way we are living and then afterwards we weep. There are so many bugs and fleas we sleep with cotton in our ears. ... In all this village there are only two houses made of wood. Everyone lives in mud huts." Mowrer, Arrest and Exile, pp. 139-140.

19 The Soviets claimed as citizens all Polish Jews and other minority groups who had lived in Poland, such as Ukrainians and Bylorussians; only Polish nationals could keep their citizenships.

20 The Soviets, like the Tsars, considered Jews a "problem" to be solved, especially after the Revolution. The Communists viewed Jews as petty-bourgeois exploiters, as "middlemen" and "class enemies," and most Jews lost their livelihoods as the Communists eliminated all small businesses. Ideology dictated that Jews be turned into farmers and workers. Birobijan was founded by the Communists in 1928 as the Jewish National District and became an Autonomous Region in 1934. There were several reasons for its founding but one of the main ones was to colonize an area into which Chinese had been infiltrating–Birobijan is north of Manchuria–and create a buffer state. The harshness of the climate, minimal amenities, and lack of infrastructure was so well known that few Russians would settle there, and most of the Jews forced to go there left.

21 The Russo-Finnish War lasted from November 30, 1939 to March 12, 1940. Finland had been independent since 1917, having broken away from Tsarist Russia at the end of World War I. As Germany became more of a threat, the Soviets demanded Finnish territory which they said they needed to protect Leningrad. The Finns refused and the USSR invaded without a declaration of war, starting the Winter War which the Soviets won but at a very high cost in men. For this action, the Soviet Union was expelled from the League of Nations in December.

22 In the first weeks after the Germans invaded Poland, Lublin was crammed with refugee Jews. The English journalist Claire Hollingworth wrote that, "Even here, the courage and tenacity of the Jewish race produced incidents, humorous and touching: A Swiss journalist was walking down the main street, hungry, having looked everywhere for food. Meeting an elderly Jew, he thought that the man might be able to advise him. "'I wonder if you can tell me, is there anywhere I can get food?'" he said. "'Food. No, no, there's nowhere here you can get food,'" the Jew answered gravely. Then a smile came to his face. "'But here,' he said, "'I have some beautiful foreign stamps. Are you interested?'" The Three Weeks' War in Poland (London: Duckworth, 1940), p. 140.

23 The people of both America and Britain sympathised with Japan during the Russo-Japanese War (1904-5), largely because of the Tsarist anti-Semitic policies which had led to many horrendous pogroms. When Japan needed money for armaments, Jacob Schiff, the Jewish President of the American banking firm of Kuhn, Loeb & Co., secured loans for Japan in collaboration with British bankers. (Schiff was decorated by Edward VII for his help.) The war cost Japan about one thousand million dollars, more than half this amount being lent by the banks of Great Britain and America. The result was that the Japanese had great respect for Jews (few of whom they had ever seen) even while they were allies of the Germans, and some 2,000 Jews who had struggled to get to Japan were taken in.

24 There had been a Jewish colony in Shanghai since the 1840s, the population increasing after

the pogroms which followed the Russian Revolution in which perhaps 200,000 Jews were killed. When Japan conquered Shanghai in 1937, the city remained open to refugee Jews for a long time, and eventually 25,000 were taken in, including some who had gone to Japan but were unable to get visas to any other country.

25 Canada had a very poor record of admitting Jews during the 1930s. Chaim Goldberg did not know the tremendous difficulty the Polish Government had to get visas to Canada for the Polish Jewish potential soldiers in Japan. The Director of Immigration in Canada, Frederick Blair, did everything he could to prevent any Jews from entering the country for any purpose. The Polish Ambassador to Japan, Wiktor Podoski, worked hard to get Canadian visas in spite of Blair's refusal to believe the young men were coming to join the Polish army. Through an error the Canadian charge d'affaires in Tokyo issued 120 visas and "By July 1941 small numbers of Jews had begun to arrive in Canada from Japan ... the first ship of some 21 Jews from Japan landing in Vancouver on June 18," Irving Abella and Harold Troper, None is Too Many, p. 90.

26 Tailoring in Poland was almost entirely a Jewish business. It was seasonal, and there was seldom enough work for a full year; even before the Depression there was only about 35 weeks of work.

27 The Ottoman Empire, which had ruled Palestine, collapsed after World War I, and in 1920 Great Britain was given the League of Nations Mandate over Palestine. "The four fundamental obligations of the Mandate ... were listed: (1) to protect and provide access to the Holy Places; (2) to establish in Palestine a national home for the Jewish people, and to facilitate Jewish immigration and a close settlement by Jews on the land; (3) to ensure that, in doing this, the rights of other sections of the population were not prejudiced; (4) to lead the country to self-governing institutions." Robert Kee, 1939: The World We Left Behind (1984; London: Penguin, 1989) p. 231.

Jews needed immigration papers from the British to enter Palestine, but these were limited and many people went illegally. If the British found an illegal immigrant, they reduced the quota for the year.

28 General Wladyslaw Sikorski (1881-1943) was a soldier who served with Pilsudski after World War I. During the early years of Polish independence, he had been Prime Minister and Minister of War. He set up a Polish Government-in-Exile in Paris in September 1939, and then in London after France capitulated in June 1940, where he was Commander-in-Chief of the Polish forces. The Ambassador to London of the Polish Government-in-Exile, Count Edward Raczynski, wrote, "This catastrophe (the death of Sikorski)–coming at a turning-point of the war, ... and when vital decisions require to be taken in consultation with us–is a bewildering visitation of providence; so much so, that Poles everywhere suspect the hand, not of Providence, but of a felonious enemy." In Allied London (London: Weidenfeld & Nicolson, 1962), p. 132. But there seems to be no evidence that Sikorski's death was other than accidental.

29 Russian-born Joseph Trumpeldor (1880-1920), a decorated officer in the Tsar's army, lost his left hand in the Russo-Japanese War. He went to Palestine in 1912, supported the British during World War I, and returned to Palestine in 1919, where he organized the defence of several Jewish settlements. In 1920 Arabs attacked the settlement he was defending, Tel Hai *("Hill of Life")*, killing Trumpeldor and seven others defending the settlement. All eight are buried at Tel Hai, where a sculptured lion marks their grave. He became a hero to pioneer Jewish youth.

30 The Haganah was a Jewish militia organized in 1921 after the first Arab attacks on Jewish settlements. During the 1930s, when German and Italian money was supporting the Arabs (who were fighting the British), the British began to help arm and train the Jewish group. After the war the Haganah helped those Jews in Europe who had survived to get to Palestine, mostly illegally, since the British still would not let them in.

31 In August 1941, the invading Germans found the bodies of around four thousand apparently murdered Polish officers in the Katyn woods in central western Russia. The Soviets put the entire blame on the Germans (though the Germans had not reached that far yet), and continued to do so until in 1990 Mikhail Gorbachev finally admitted, officially, that the approximately 15,000 murdered Polish officers–another ten thousand bodies were later found at two other places–all prisoners of war, had been shot on Stalin's orders in the spring of 1940. Stalin denounced the Polish Government-in-Exile for accusing the Soviets of the crime and broke off relations.

32 SS stands for Schutzstaffel *("protection detachments").* They were the Blackshirts, led by Heinrich Himmler, the Nazi Party's army responsible for maintaining the regime and destroying all "enemies of the state," especially Jews. They ran the concentration and extermination camps and were known for ruthlessly killing prisoners-of-war. Poles and Polish Jews had a particular hatred for the SS, who were in charge of the torture and killings in Poland during the German invasion in September 1939. Among other duties, the SS packed and shipped to the Reichsbank the "gold and silver coins, jewellery, dental gold, spectacles and banknotes, in neat packages and larger crates, ... amounting to some $14.5 million in all," taken from those sent to the concentration and death camps. A. J. Sherman, review of Arthur L. Smith, Jr., Hitler's Gold: The Story of the Nazi War Loot (Oxford: Berg, 1990), TLS March 23-29, 1990, p. 313.

33 A Jew needed about $5,000 US or the equivalent. Few Polish Jews had this much, but many German Jews did.

34 As 30,000 Polish boys from Detroit and Chicago had done in World War I. General Sikorski hoped to recruit from the 4,000,000 Americans of Polish descent, but in World War II they joined the American Army.

35 On May 10, 1941, Rudolf Hess, Hitler's colleague and confidant for nearly 20 years, parachuted into Scotland and was interned. It was never completely clear why he came; after the war he was tried as a war criminal and imprisoned in Spandau, where he died. Gilbert, Second World War, p. 181.

36 Silesia, in central Europe, is a region long fought over, with a lengthy and complex history. After World War I, it was divided among Poland, Czechoslavakia, and Germany, but that satisfied no one, each country continuing to press claims for more territory.

37 One of the major battles of the war in northern Europe. Massive numbers of German soldiers were encircled near the French city of Falaise, and it took large numbers of English, Canadians, and Poles (of the First Polish Armoured Division) to close the Gap and prevent their escape. The Gap was closed August 20-21, 1944.

38 Nor did the English trust the French. At the beginning of the war the English sent over a British Expeditionary Force which was sent north of the Maginot Line. The American reporter Drew Middleton later wrote, "As they waited, the British became increasingly concerned over the bearing and morale of the French soldiers. Unkempt, unshaven, surly, they seemed to have little interest in the defense of their own country. British officers who dined with their French counterparts reported that their hosts kept repeating the phrase, 'Rather Hitler than Blum,' a reference to the Jewish former Socialist Premier of France.'" "On the night of June 16 [1940], we were told that the French had asked the British Government to release them from the agreement not to make a separate peace, which it did." "The World Has Never Been Quite the Same," The New York Times Magazine September 3, 1989, pp. 30, 46.

The French "saved their own gold reserves by obligingly handing over to the Germans Belgian and Polish gold confided to the Banque de France for safekeeping." A. J. Sherman, review of Arthur L. Smith, Jr., Hitler's Gold: The Story of the Nazi War Loot, Times Literary Supplement, March 23-29, 1990, p. 313.

The French did fight, of course as did the Czechs. But Chaim Goldberg felt that the Poles had put up a much greater fight against the Germans than did the French, who were allies of the Poles and who had signed a treaty to give the Poles help if the Germans attacked. After France fell in June 1940, of the French servicemen "marooned in England after the armistice of June [1940] only 7,000 soldiers and sailors had donned the Cross of Lorraine and of those the largest contingent was a demi-brigade of the Foreign Legion, by definition not French in nationality. And even fewer Frenchmen, however strong their anti-German feeling, had shown themselves ready to take the yet more extreme step of quitting France to join de Gaulle in England." Keegan, Six Armies in Normandy, p. 299.

39 Herb Gray has been the Liberal Member of Parliament for Windsor West since 1962; in 1993 he was named Solicitor General in the Liberal Government. His mother used to send packages of goodies to Jewish soldiers in the Canadian and Polish Armies.

40 On May 13, 1939, the German liner St. Louis left Hamburg with 930 Jewish refugees, 734 holding U.S. quota numbers and all having Cuban landing certificates. But the Cubans refused

all but 22 and ordered the ship to leave; even though American Jews offered a million dollars in guarantees, the U.S. and various Latin American countries refused to take them. Finally, Britain took 287, and Holland and Belgium took the rest, but they shortly came under German rule.

41 Three thousand seven hundred "Dutch were killed fighting for the Germans, mostly in combat units of the Waffen SS, for which the Germans recruited widely and with special enthusiasm among those of 'aryan' stock whom they encouraged to join in defending the 'new Europe' against the Bolsheviks." R.A.C. Parker, Struggle for Survival: The History of the Second World War (Oxford/New York: Oxford University Press, 1989), p. 284.

But while there was a Dutch National Socialist Party, there was also an underground group which, among many other valuable and honourable deeds, saved Jewish children and helped Allied soldiers to escape. See Robert Kee, 1945: The World We Fought For (Boston: Little, Brown and Company, 1985), pp. 172-4.

42 Among the German "secret weapons" was the V-1 (the V standing for "Vergeltung" or "Reprisal") known to the British as the "Buzz Bomb" or "Doodlebug." The V-1 was first launched against England on June 13, 1944; the last fell on March 29, 1945. They were fired from a number of places on the coast. The V-1 had a warhead of one ton, a range of 200 miles, and flew 400 mph; the V-2 was more deadly. These were indiscriminate weapons, dropping anywhere, killing thousands in London, Antwerp, and Liege, and often misfiring and landing on Germans. The fear of the rockets was so great that Prime Minister Winston Churchill "was prepared, after consultation with the United States and the USSR, to threaten the enemy with large-scale gas attacks in retaliation, should such a course appear profitable." Martin Gilbert, Second World War (Toronto: Stoddart Publishing Co., Ltd., 1989), p. 557.

43 The Siegfried Line was a line of fortifications put up by Germany in the 1930s partly in response to France's Maginot Line; it was to run from Switzerland to Luxembourg, but was dismantled in 1940 after France fell, later being partially rebuilt in 1944. The Germans called it the West Wall.

44 This act was not unusual:

(1) On March 4, 19454, toward the end of the war, Churchill along with Montgomery, Brooke, and other generals visited the troops near the recently taken Siegfried Line. "As the entourage moved on to the Siegfried Line, Churchill emulated the Jocks in giving the historic gesture of contempt for his enemy, the prospect of which he had been savouring throughout the long years of war. It was thus described:

"The Prime Minister climbed out of his car and walked solemnly to the line of 'dragon's teeth.' Unbuttoning his fly, he turned to the assembled officers.

"'Gentlemen,' he said sonorously. 'I'd like to ask you to join me. Let us all urinate on the great West Wall of Germany.' He wagged a finger at the photographers, who were aiming their cameras, and called out, 'This is one of those operations connected with this great war which must not be reproduced graphically.'

"[Field-Marshal Sir Alan] Brooke stood next to the prime minister. 'I shall never forget the childish grin of intense satisfaction that spread all over his face as he looked down at the critical moment.'" W. Denis and Shelagh Whitaker, Rhineland: The Battle to End The War (Toronto: Stoddart, 1989), p. 272.

(2) Just after the war, the American journalist I.F. Stone and a Red Cross executive borrowed a jeep and drove to Berchtesgaden, Hitler's house high in the mountains in Bavaria. "The Hitler house was a wreck. Allied bombers and souvenir hunters had left little behind them. The walls were covered with the handwriting of GI's and the Mogen Dovids of American Jewish soldiers. On the second floor, in the huge victory hall, the whole side of one wall had held one great window overlooking the Alps. The view made megalomania almost inescapable for anyone who lived there. Solemnly I committed a primitive act of contempt." Underground to Palestine, p. 115.

45 Chaim Goldberg: "Here in Windsor I saw a man with a book and I said, 'Mister, I've seen you carrying a Polish book, show me that book! I want to see it!' and I find Gorelik was in it! The book was called *Ucieczki Kuwolnosci*, means 'memories of Polish people who ran away from occupied Poland to freedom.' I said, 'Did you know the men who wrote this?' And he answered

me, 'They have been neighbours of mine in the old country and they sent me that book.' I said, 'Listen, I'll give the money, right away they'll give you another book, he was with me in the regiment.' The book was about how Gorelik escaped to Holland where he was a prisoner-of-war. The underground got him to a farm and put him under the hay and smuggled him out from that farm. The Germans have been watching, they went through the hay with wires but they didn't find him and the underground got him out at night into Belgium, he got into Lotharingia, to France, and he escaped through the Pyrenees to Spain. They caught him there and put him in a concentration camp, Camp Ebro. He and others organized a tunnel–the Spaniards treat them very bad–he told everybody, 'Take a spoonful of dirt in your pocket.' They got out, captured about ten Spanish soldiers, took away from them their weapons and they marched down to Barcelona. (Franco was with Hitler, mixed up fifty-fifty.) They came through Gibraltar, he came to the Polish Army, he was with me, a fine officer, but I haven't seen him since the army." The book is by Ryszard Dylinski, Jerzy Korczak, and Nieczyslaw Skapski, Ucieczki Kuwolnosci (Poznanskie, 1980).

46 K. Jamar recalls these captured Polish women, too: "A 2nd Lt. Papee rushed into the room of the Regimental Commander, saying, 'Sir, we are wasting time here, when a few steps away the Germans are keeping hundreds of Polish women in a concentration camp.'" Jamar goes on to recount how the liberated women poured out of their hutments, dressed in "Polish forage caps with red-and-white flashes, trousers and high boots, American skirts and uniforms, belts, NCO's and officers badges on the caps and shoulder straps... . tears were flowing down all faces, exhausted with their experiences during the Warsaw Rising and the imprisonment in camps. They were tears of happiness.... At last the long prayed-for freedom had come. Freedom brought to them by Poles, by General Maczek's tanks, by the 1st Polish Armoured Division." With the Tanks of the Ist Polish Armoured Division, p. 298.

47 Lidice was a town in Czechoslovakia destroyed–men, women and children–by Germans in 1942 in retaliation for the killing of a sadistic and vicious Nazi official.

48 The Allies put almost two dozen high-ranking Nazis on trial at Nuremberg, Germany, November 1945 to October 1946, charging them with "Crimes against humanity."

49 In August 1944, Churchill decided that "Jewish soldiers in the Allied Armies, and above all in Palestine, could serve in a specifically Jewish fighting unit, to be known as the Jewish Brigade Group. This force, Churchill explained to Roosevelt, would constitute 'what you would call a regimental combat team,' and he added: 'This will give great satisfaction to the Jews when it is published and surely they of all other races have the right to strike at the Germans as a recognizable body. They wish to have their own flag which is a Star of David on a white background with two light blue bars." Martin Gilbert, Second World War, p. 576. The Jewish Brigade was active in getting supplies and transportation one way or another for Jewish refugees on their (illegal) way to Palestine.

50 The Six-Day War, June 5-11, 1967, Israel against Egypt, Jordan, and Syria. Israeli soldiers routed the Egyptian forces and pushed into the Sinai to Cairo; they took Jerusalem and the West Bank of the Jordan River from Jordan.

51 At a meeting of High Commissioners in London on April 12, 1946, each Commissioner was asked to discuss Polish immigration with his home government. Canada's Vincent Massey was there and "surprised some of those present with the vehemence of his anti-Polish remarks. Poles were, he allowed, only slightly better than Jews." Canada did admit four thousand Polish war veterans but "Jewish members of the Polish army were to be carefully screened out." Irving Abella and Harold Troper, None Is Too Many (Toronto: Lester & Orpen Dennys, 1982), pp. 218-220.

Selected Bibliography

Abella, Irving, and Harold Troper. None Is Too Many. Toronto: Lester & Orpen Dennys, 1982. How the Canadian government refused to take in Jews in the 1930s.

Abramovitch, Raphael. The Vanished World. New York: Forward Association, 1947. Picture Album.

Ainsztein, Reuben. Jewish Resistance in Nazi-Occupied Eastern Europe. London: P. Elek, 1974.

Arad, Yitzhak. Ghetto in Flames: The Struggle and Destruction of the Jews in Vilna in the Holocaust. Yad Vashem: Jerusalem, 1980.

Ascherson, Neal. The Struggles for Poland. London: Michael Joseph, 1987. Popular history, illustrated.

Bor-Komorowski, T. The Secret Army. London: Victor Gollancz Ltd., 1950. Polish underground, by its leader.

Coutouvidis, John, and Jaime Reynolds. Poland 1939-1947. New York: Holmes & Meier, 1986.

Davies, Norman. God's Playground, a History of Poland. 2 vols. (New York: Columbia University Press, 1982.

Dawidowicz, Lucy S. From that Place and Time: A Memoir 1938-1947. New York: W.W. Norton, 1989. Memoir of her year in Vilna.

________. The War Against the Jews 1933-1945. New York: Holt, Rinehart & Winston, 1975.

Engel, David. In The Shadow of Auschwitz: The Polish Government- in-Exile and the Jews, 1939-1945. Chapel Hill: University of North Carolina Press, 1987.

Garlinski, Jozef. Poland in the Second World War. London: Macmillan, 1985.

Gilbert, Martin. Second World War. Toronto: Stoddart Publishing Company, Ltd., 1989.

________. The Holocaust: The History of the Jews of Europe During the Second World War. New York: Henry Holt & Co., 1987.

________. Jewish History Atlas. London: Weidenfeld and Nicolson, 1969.

________. Russian History Atlas. London: Weidenfeld and Nicholson, 1972.

Gutman, Yisrael, Ezra Mendelsohn, Jehuda Reinharz, and Chone Shmeruk, eds. The Jews of Poland Between Two World Wars. London: University Press of New England, 1989.

Hautzig, Esther. The Endless Steppe. London: Hamish Hamilton, 1968. With her family and many other middle-class Jews she was taken as a child from Vilna to Siberia by the Soviets.

________. Remember Who You Are: Stories About Being Jewish. New York: Crown Publishers, Inc., 1990. What she found when she returned to Poland after the war.

Heller, Celia. On the Edge of Destruction: Jews of Poland between the Two World Wars. New York: Columbia University Press, 1976.

Heppner, Ernest G. Shanghai Refuge: A Memoir of the World War II Jewish Ghetto. Lincoln, Neb.: University of Nebraska Press, 1993. Memoir of a Jew who with his mother survived in Shanghai during the war.

Kaufman, Michael. Mad Dreams, Saving Graces: Poland: A Nation in Conspiracy. New York: Random House, 1989. A New York Times journalist and his father, a Polish Jew, return to Poland.

Karski, Jan. Story of a Secret State. Boston: Houghton Mifflin Company, 1944. A famous book about Poland and Polish Jews under the Nazis.

Kee, Robert. The World We Left Behind: A Chronicle of the Year 1939. London: Sphere Books Ltd., 1984.

Keegan, John. Six Armies in Normandy: From D-Day to the Liberation of Paris. New York: Viking Press, 1982. The Polish Army is one of the six.

Korbonski, Stefan. The Polish Underground State: A Guide to the Underground 1939-1945. East European Quarterly, Boulder: distr. Columbia University Press, 1978.

Kugelmass, Jack, and Jonathan Boyarin, trans. and ed. From a Ruined Garden: The Memorial Books of Polish Jewry. New York: Schocken Books, 1983. The survivors of many small Polish Jewish towns compiled these books as memorials to those who did not survive.

Kukiel, Lt.-General Marian. Six Years of Struggle for Independence. Newtown: Montgomeryshire Printing Co., Ltd., 1947. First-person account of the German onslaught on Poland; Polish forces in the war.

Laffan, M. "Weimar and Versailles: German Foreign Policy 1919-1933," in M. Laffan, ed. The Burden of German History 1919-1945. London: Methuen, 1988.

Levin, Nora. The Holocaust: The Destruction of European Jewry 1933-1945. New York: Schocken, 1968.

Lukas, Richard C. Forgotten Holocaust: The Poles under German Occupation 1939-1944. New York: Hippocrene Books, 1986.

Mendelsohn, Ezra. The Jews of East Central Europe Between the World Wars. Bloomington, Indiana: Indiana University Press, 1983.

Niezabitowska, Malgorzata, photographs by Thomasz Tomaszewski. Remnants: The Last Jews of Poland. Trans. Williams Brand and Hanna Doboziewicz. New York: Friendly Press, Inc, 1986. Only about five thousand Jews survive in Poland, mostly very old. Well written, beautiful photographs.

Overy, Richard, with Andrew Wheatcroft. The Road to War. London: Macmillan London Limited, 1989. The authors try to look at the actions of each country without hindsight.

Parker, R. A. C. Struggle for Survival: The History of the Second World War. Oxford/New York: Oxford University Press, 1989.

Rabinowicz, Henry M. The Legacy of Polish Jewry: A History of Polish Jews in the Inter-War Years 1919-1939. New York/London, Thomas Yoseloff, 1965.

Read, Anthony, and David Fisher. The Deadly Embrace: Hitler, Stalin, and the Nazi-Soviet Pace 1939-1941. New York: W. W. Norton & Company, 1988.

Reitlinger, Gerald. The Final Solution, the Attempt To Exterminate the Jews of Europe 1939-45. South Brunswick, N.Y.: T. Yoseloff, 1968.

Sachar, Abram L. Sufferance is the Badge: The Jew in the Contemporary World. New York and London: Alfred A. Knopf, 1940. A portrait of Polish Jews in the late 1930s.

Salsitz, Norman, as told to Richard Skolnik. A Jewish Boyhood in Poland. Syracuse: Syracuse University Press, 1992. Salsitz was born in 1920.

________. and Amalie Petranker Salsitz. Against All Odds: A Tale of Two Survivors. New York: Holocaust Library, 1990. He survived in the woods and then as a partisan; she survived in the city with Polish Catholic identity papers.

Snyder, Louis L. Historical Guide to World War II. Westport, Conn.: Greenwood Press, 1982. A one-volume encyclopedia.

Tokayer, Marvin, and Mary Swartz. The Fugu Plan: The Untold Story of the Japanese and the Jews During World War II. New York & London: Paddington Press Ltd., 1979. A little-known story.

Vago, Bella, and George L. Mosse, eds. Jews and Non-Jews in Eastern Europe 1918-1945. Jerusalem: Israel Universities Press, 1974.

Vardys, V. Stanley, ed. Lithuania under the Soviets 1940-1965: Aggression Soviet Style 1939-1940. New York: Frederick Praeger, 1965.

Vishniac, Roman. Polish Jews. New York: Schocken Books, 1947. Picture Album.

Watt, Donald Cameron. How War Came: The Immediate Origins of the Second World War, 1938-1939. London: Pantheon, 1989.

Wynot, Edward D., Jr. Warsaw Between the World Wars: Profile of the Capital City in a Developing Land, 1918-1939. East European Monographs, No. CXXIX, Boulder (New York: distr. Columbia University Press, 1983.

Zamoyski, Adam. The Polish Way: A Thousand-Year History of the Poles and Their Culture. New York: Franklin Watts, 1988.

Above: The Goldberg Family: (front) Mother, Cyna, Father; (back) Scholem, Pearl, Chaim.

Right: Chaim Goldberg, aged 19.

Far right: Isaak Ruchleimer, in Lithuania, 1940.

Chaim and Scholem, New Year's card, around 1936-37.

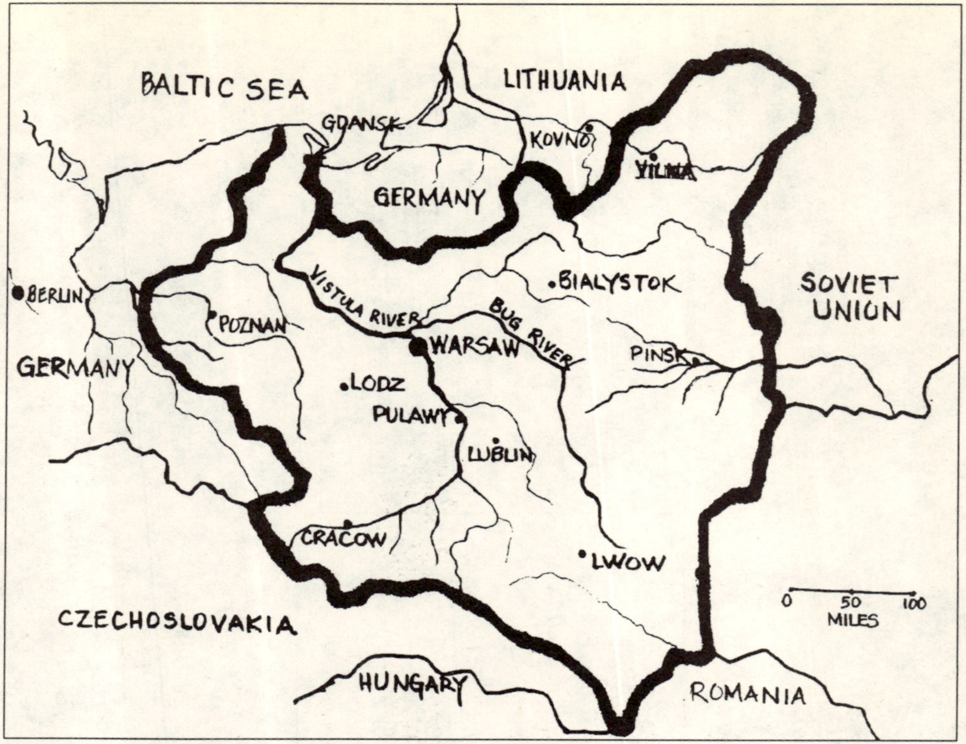

Poland: 1920-1939

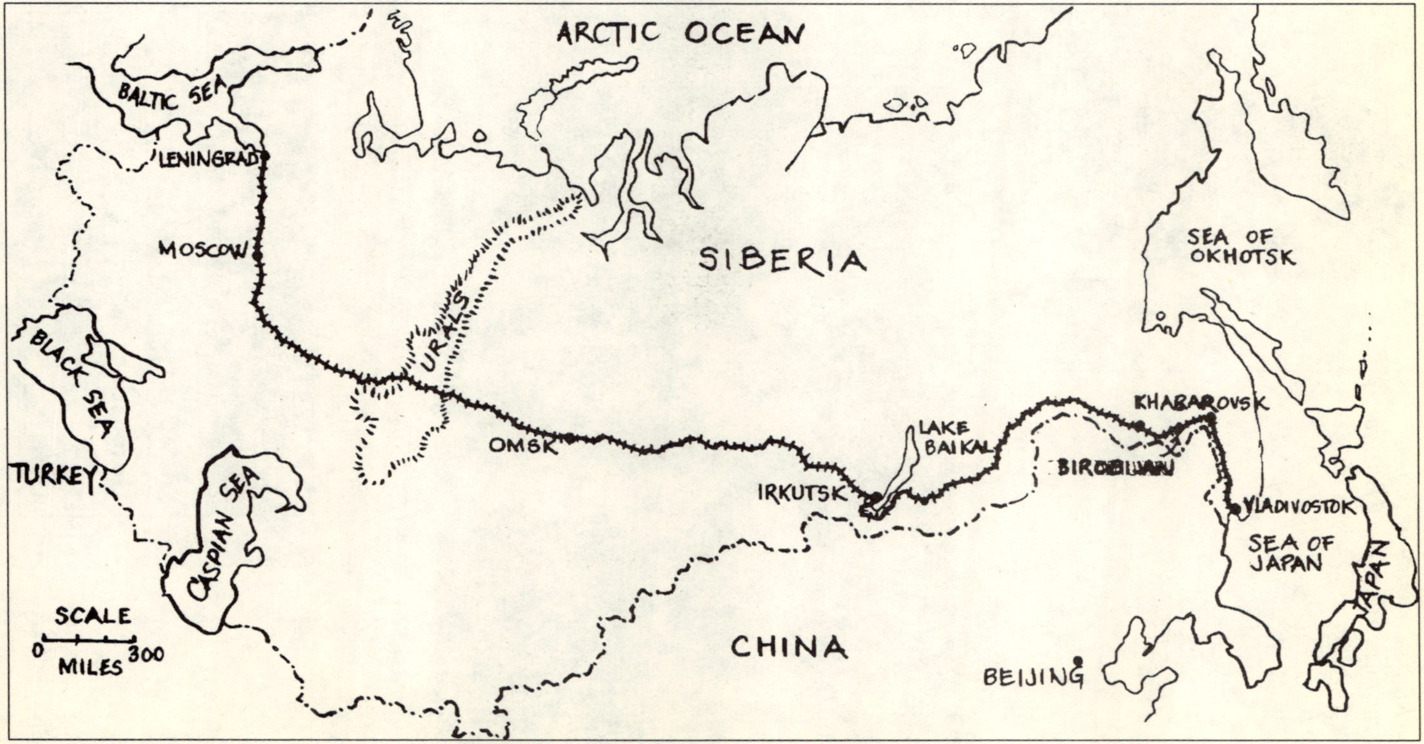

TRANS SIBERIAN RAILROAD

Avram Richter, a watchmaker, who made the false papers which enabled Chaim Goldberg to go across the U.S.S.R.

Polish Jewish men embark on the Hikawa Maru, headed for Canada and the Polish Army.

Chaim Goldberg's baggage ticket on the Hikawa-Maru.

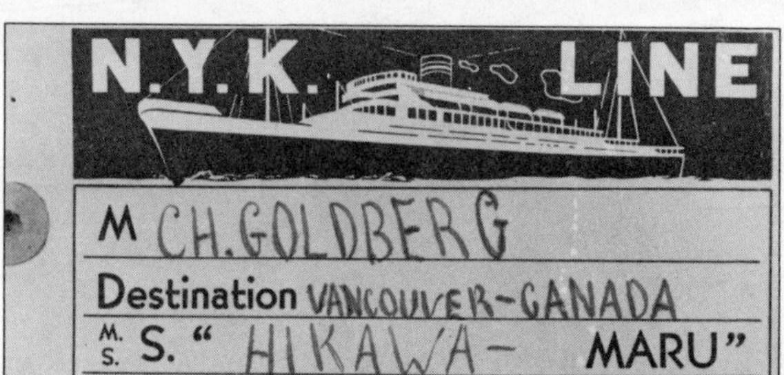

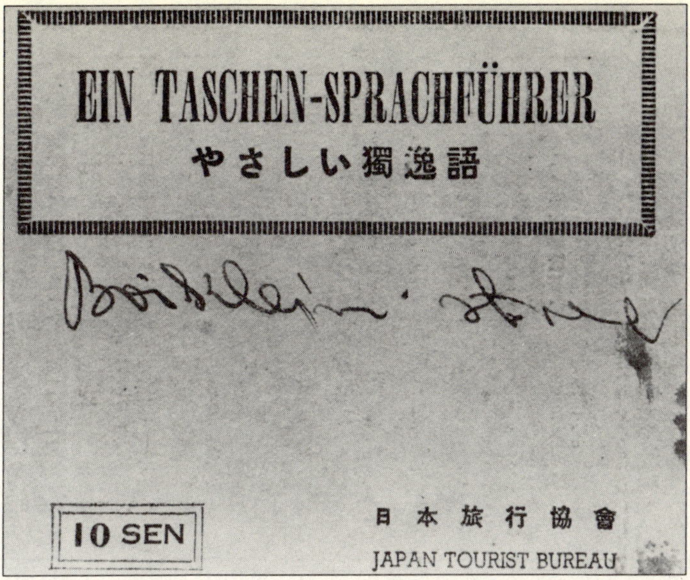

EIN TASCHEN-SPRACHFÜHRER
やさしい獨逸語

10 SEN

日本旅行協會
JAPAN TOURIST BUREAU

German-Japanese book Chaim Goldberg bought in Japan.

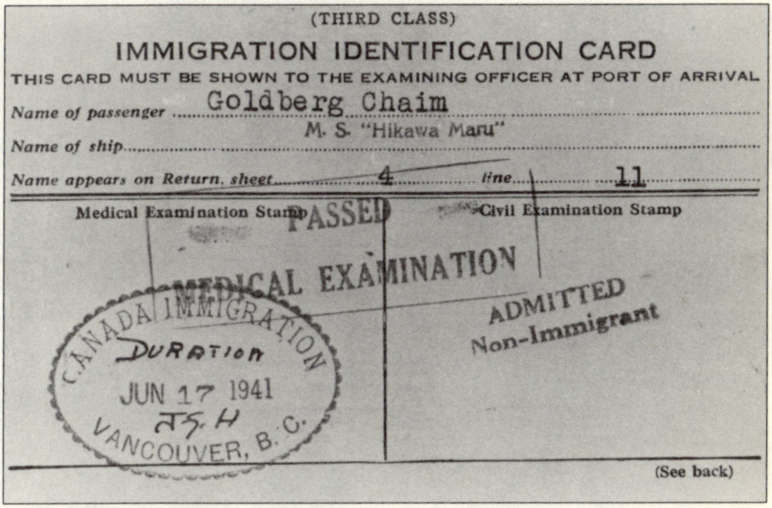

(THIRD CLASS)

IMMIGRATION IDENTIFICATION CARD

THIS CARD MUST BE SHOWN TO THE EXAMINING OFFICER AT PORT OF ARRIVAL

Name of passenger Goldberg Chaim

Name of ship M. S. "Hikawa Maru"

Name appears on Return. sheet 4 line 11

Medical Examination Stamp PASSED MEDICAL EXAMINATION

Civil Examination Stamp

CANADA IMMIGRATION
DURATION
JUN 17 1941
VANCOUVER, B. C.

ADMITTED
Non-Immigrant

(See back)

Entrance card coming from Japan, labelled "Non-Immigrant".

In Japan: Chaim and Isaak (at left) in Kobe, 1941.

Chaim in uniform.

Leo Verboecke, Head of the Ghent Resistance, taken in 1952, when he was a minister in the Belgian government. Chaim Goldberg had met him during the war in Ghent.

Polish-Silesian soldiers from Rommel's army who joined the Polish Army; Chaim Goldberg is on the left.

Front left, kneeling, a Polish orphan boy the soldiers picked up and took care of until the war was over; Chaim Goldberg is third from left, the rest of the soldiers are from Rommel's army, who surrendered at El Alamein and later joined the Polish Army.

CORPORAL GOLDBERG IN GERMANY, IN A TRUCK DURING THE WAR.

RABBI KLEPFISZ, THE RABBI OF THE REGIMENT, OFFICIATING AT THE FUNERAL OF LEO CHERTOK IN BREDA.

Bergen Belsen, 1945.

A picture Chaim sent to Ruth in Windsor, Ontario, the woman who became his wife when he immigrated to Canada after the war.

Chaim Goldberg, above right, with a fellow soldier, "a good sniper" who had come from Russia, through Iran, to Palestine, and then to Scotland.

Chaim Goldberg's jeep "had thousands of miles, and 33 bullets".

German prisoners of the Polish Army near Oldenburg, Germany.

Dinner time: Schimanofsky Stefan is on the left, Chaim Goldberg in the middle.

After the regiment had taken Breda, sent to Ruth in Windsor, Ontario.

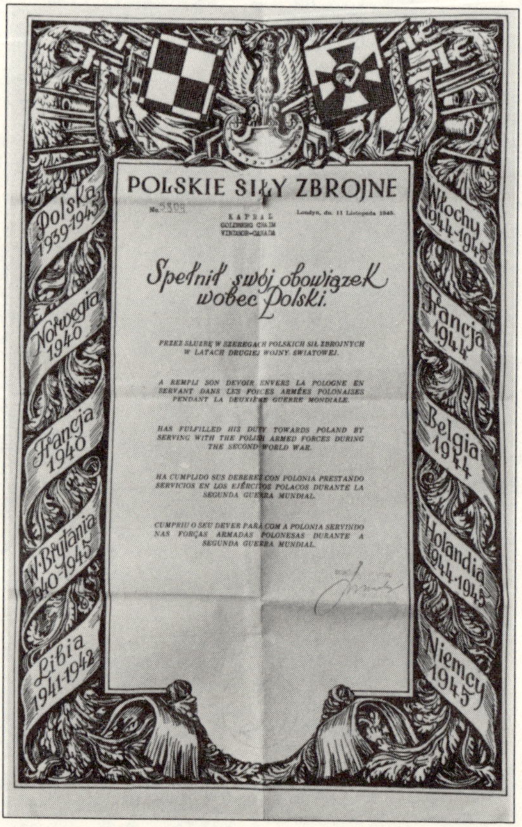

Polska 1939-1945
Norwegia 1940
Francja 1940
W. Brytania 1940-1945
Libia 1941-1942
Włochy 1944-1945
Francja 1944
Belgia 1944
Holandia 1944-1945
Niemcy 1945

POLSKIE SIŁY ZBROJNE

No. 5309 — Londyn, dn. 11 Listopada 1945.

KAPRAL
GOLDBERG CHAIM
WINDSOR—CANADA

Spełnił swój obowiązek wobec Polski.

PRZEZ SŁUŻBĘ W SZEREGACH POLSKICH SIŁ ZBROJNYCH W LATACH DRUGIEJ WOJNY ŚWIATOWEJ.

A REMPLI SON DEVOIR ENVERS LA POLOGNE EN SERVANT DANS LES FORCES ARMÉES POLONAISES PENDANT LA DEUXIÈME GUERRE MONDIALE.

HAS FULFILLED HIS DUTY TOWARDS POLAND BY SERVING WITH THE POLISH ARMED FORCES DURING THE SECOND WORLD WAR.

HA CUMPLIDO SUS DEBERES CON POLONIA PRESTANDO SERVICIOS EN LOS EJÉRCITOS POLACOS DURANTE LA SEGUNDA GUERRA MUNDIAL.

CUMPRIU O SEU DEVER PARA COM A POLONIA SERVINDO NAS FORÇAS ARMADAS POLONESAS DURANTE A SEGUNDA GUERRA MUNDIAL.

Discharge from the Polish Army in five languages, given in Scotland.

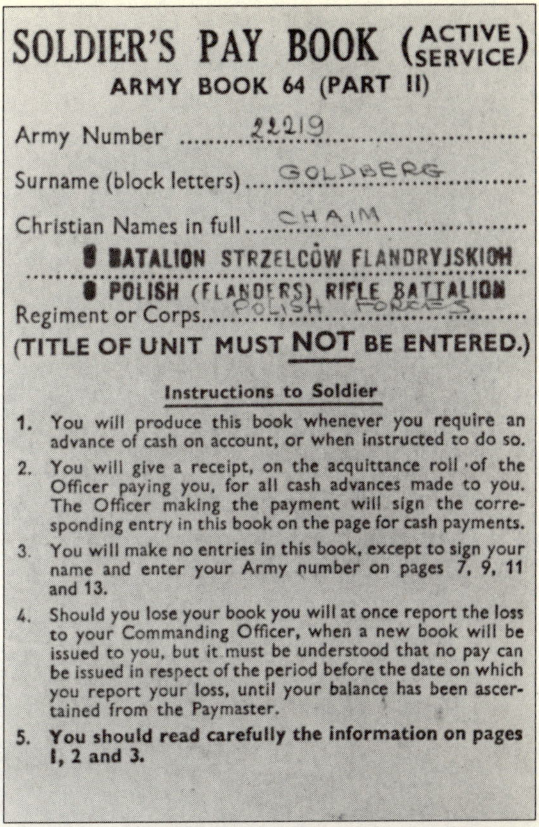
SOLDIER'S PAY BOOK (ACTIVE SERVICE)

ARMY BOOK 64 (PART II)

Army Number ....22219........

Surname (block letters) ....GOLDBERG........

Christian Names in full ....CHAIM........

8 BATALION STRZELCÓW FLANDRYJSKICH

8 POLISH (FLANDERS) RIFLE BATTALION

Regiment or Corps........POLISH FORCES........

(TITLE OF UNIT MUST NOT BE ENTERED.)

Instructions to Soldier

1. You will produce this book whenever you require an advance of cash on account, or when instructed to do so.
2. You will give a receipt, on the acquittance roll of the Officer paying you, for all cash advances made to you. The Officer making the payment will sign the corresponding entry in this book on the page for cash payments.
3. You will make no entries in this book, except to sign your name and enter your Army number on pages 7, 9, 11 and 13.
4. Should you lose your book you will at once report the loss to your Commanding Officer, when a new book will be issued to you, but it must be understood that no pay can be issued in respect of the period before the date on which you report your loss, until your balance has been ascertained from the Paymaster.
5. **You should read carefully the information on pages 1, 2 and 3.**

The Polish soldiers had the same pay book as the British Army.

Men with whom Chaim Goldberg served in the Polish Army: (from left) Goldstin, unknown, Ludwig Kleiner, Ismar Glassman.

Polish soldiers, taken in Holland during the war.

Chaim with Mr. and Mrs. Melrose, in Melrose, Scotland.

Right: Temporary identification paper given by the Polish government in Kaunas, Lithuania, 21 December, 1939.

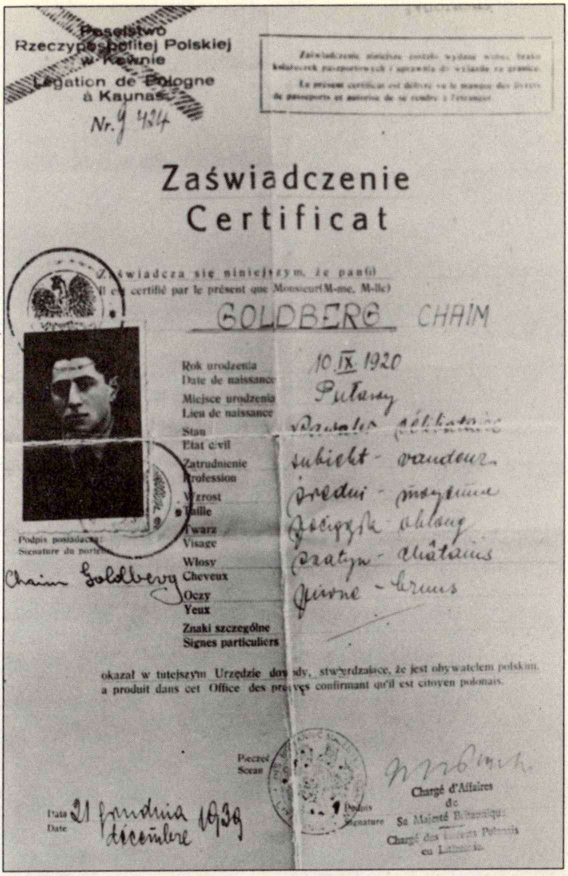

Poselstwo Rzeczypospolitej Polskiej w Kownie
Légation de Pologne à Kaunas
Nr. 9 424

Zaświadczenie niniejsze zostało wydane wobec braku książeczek paszportowych i uprawnia do wyjazdu za granicę.
Le présent certificat est délivré vu le manque des livrets de passeports et autorise de se rendre à l'étranger.

Zaświadczenie
Certificat

Zaświadcza się niniejszym, że pan(i)
Il est certifié par le présent que Monsieur(M-me, M-lle)
GOLDBERG CHAIM

Rok urodzenia / Date de naissance: 10.IX.1920
Miejsce urodzenia / Lieu de naissance: Pułtusk
Stan / Etat civil: kawaler - célibataire
Zatrudnienie / Profession: subiekt - vendeur
Wzrost / Taille: średni - moyenne
Twarz / Visage: pociągła - oblong
Włosy / Cheveux: szatyn - châtains
Oczy / Yeux: piwne - bruns
Znaki szczególne / Signes particuliers

Podpis posiadacza: / Signature du porteur: Chaim Goldberg

okazał w tutejszym Urzędzie dowody, stwierdzające, że jest obywatelem polskim.
a produit dans cet Office des preuves confirmant qu'il est citoyen polonais.

Pieczęć / Sceau

Data / Date: 21 grudnia 1939 / décembre

Podpis / Signature
Chargé d'Affaires de Sa Majesté Britannique
Chargé des Intérêts Polonais en Lituanie

Below: Polish government document of February 8, 1945 showing that Chaim Goldberg's entire family was taken to Treblinka in 1943 and murdered there. The top half of the document is in Russian, the bottom half in Polish—the Soviet Union was occupying Poland.

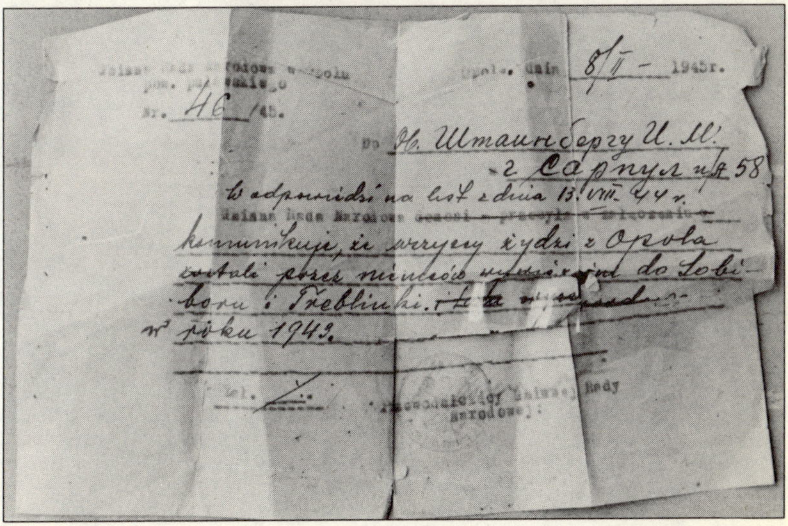

Gminna Rada Narodowa w Opolu
pow. puławskiego
Nr. 46/45.

Opole, dnia 8/II - 1945r.

Do Ж. Шмаинбергу И. М.
г. Сарнул ул. 58

W odpowiedzi na list z dnia 13.VIII.44 r.
Gminna Rada Narodowa ~~uprzejmie~~
komunikuje, że wszyscy żydzi z Opola
zostali przez niemców wywiezieni do Sobi-
boru i Treblinki. ~~...~~
w roku 1943.

Sekr.

Przewodniczący Gminnej Rady Narodowej:

Chaim Goldberg in front of his Fish Market, around 1970.

Chaim Goldberg pointing to the gravestone of his captain, Judkowiak, at the cemetery in Breda.